"Countless books have been written about prayer, but few of them teach us to pray. In *God Encounter,* Lisa Bergren invites us to reflect on a series of richly woven 'pray stories' designed to help us slow down and enter more deeply into the presence of God."

—ANN SPANGLER, best-selling author of *Women of the Bible*

"Imagine your faith deepening. Imagine a closer walk with God. Imagine prayer as a bold and creative dialogue. *God Encounter* breathes life into that imagination."

—LYNNE HINTON, author of *Garden of Faith*

"The gospel accounts give us very little, really, about the time Jesus' disciples spent with him. The down time. The hanging-around time in front of a small fire under a starlit sky. The time of intimate conversation or of mutual silence and comfortable peace. Lisa Bergren's book gives us a taste of what it might have been like to be with Jesus. Really be with him. To know. To be known. I welcome you to the reading— and the experiencing—of this wonderful book. But perhaps it should come with a warning. It could change everything."

—ROBERT WOLGEMUTH, best-selling author

"*God Encounter* brings prayer to life. You don't merely read the pages; you experience prayer as the author draws you in using multiple senses. A refreshing, engaging, moving resource."

—THOM AND JOANI SCHULTZ, authors of *The Dirt on Learning*

God Encounter

God Encounter

EXPERIENCING THE POWER
of CREATIVE PRAYER

LISA TAWN BERGREN

WATERBROOK
PRESS

GOD ENCOUNTER
PUBLISHED BY WATERBROOK PRESS
2375 Telstar Drive, Suite 160
Colorado Springs, Colorado 80920
A division of Random House, Inc.

ISBN 1-57856-638-X

Library of Congress Cataloging-in-Publication Data
Bergren, Lisa Tawn.
    God encounter : experiencing the power of creative prayer /
  Lisa Tawn Bergren.— 1st ed.
      p. cm.
    ISBN 1-57856-638-X
    1. Devotional exercises. I. Title.
  BV4832.3.B47 2002
  248.3—dc21

                                                          2002010170

Printed in the United States of America
2002—First Edition

10 9 8 7 6 5 4 3 2 1

In memory of our beloved
MADISON GRACE BERGGREN,
1996–2002,
now experiencing the
best God Encounter of all
because she knew
Jesus loved her.

Contents

Contents

Acknowledgments

Many people encouraged me along this track when I wondered if I was completely lost. God kept urging me forward. Aiding Him were my husband, Tim, and my agent, Kathryn Helmers, who could see it from the start. My pastor, Tyg Taylor, told me to quit being scared and go for it, and many friends and family—Pastor Bob Rognlien, Pastor Rick and Cheryl Crawford, Jim and Karen Grosswiler, Pastor John and Hope Bergren, Jack Cavanaugh, Gloria Dettbarn, Julie Reed, Colleen Stickel, and Barbara Richardson—gave me excellent input. Many women were subjected to trial runs of the prayers at the Trinity retreats in 2001 and 2002, and some gave me feedback along the way, especially Anita Seagraves, Margarete Seagraves, Janet Bochinski, Connie Burris, Melissa Bonser, Kim Hedstrom, and Barb Knitt—among others. Musicians Spencer Capier and Spencer Welch loaned their talents to the soundtrack portion of this project, and Anita Seagraves and Tim Bergren put many hours into the audio-visual devotional. To see and hear more of their wonderful work, log on to www.GodEncounter.com.

Introduction

OPEN YOUR HEART
TO THE HOLY

Welcome to a new way of praying or, for some of us, back to it. I was first introduced to creative prayer techniques twenty years ago.

I'll never forget that first experience in which our pastor led us through a prayer that helped me "see" Jesus for the first time, right there beside me. All of a sudden, Christ was real, touchable, and *present.*

A couple of years ago I led a Bible study on Richard Foster's phenomenal book *Prayer: Finding the Heart's True Home.* In it, he talked about using the imagination to bring God to our side. It reawakened that need in me to invite Jesus closer and to use all the creativity that the Lord had instilled in my mind to do so. Part of the result is this book. My hope is that it awakens in you that same dormant awareness that God does not have to remain distant. As when we go to the movies or find ourselves absorbed in a novel, living alongside the fictional characters, laughing and weeping with them, so can we pray in a vital, *present* fashion.

For the imaginative prayer to come to fruition for you, you must approach it as you do with any prayer—with holy expectancy and reverence. If you're used to praying with head bowed, try lying prostrate on the floor. Bored with that? Try kneeling. I myself like to spread out on my back, with arms stretched wide, palms facing up...literally open and vulnerable beneath His gaze.

I find it useful to do some relaxation and journaling to first clear my head of the distracters—anything from making a dental appointment to discussing something of depth with my husband. I sometimes begin with soothing instrumental music or a Christian song, liturgy, or hymn with great lyrics. Other times, I like to focus on Scripture. Therefore, you'll find similar suggestions that precede each prayer in this book to help calm your heart and focus your mind, but feel free to do what moves you. We are all wonderfully, creatively unique. But *do* discover what prepares your heart for an encounter with Christ.

At a loss? Try my suggestions. They might spur your mind on to other things that would be more appropriate for you.

It's important that we take the time to withdraw from the bustle of our lives—from work, television, phones, conversation—to concentrate only on God and how He's moving in our lives. Jesus routinely pulled away to do this; how can we not? I find that the longer I go without prayer and meditation time—time reserved just for Jesus and me—the harder it is to get back into the rhythm of prayer. God feels far from me, and it's because of my neglect, not His, that it feels this way. About a week back into my holy habit, I can feel Him closer, and I'm left wondering: Why is it that I forget how important this is and have to relearn this lesson again and again and again? It makes me want to throttle myself. Thank God for grace!

God understands us, you know. He sees us as fabulous, intriguing, wonderful creations that are just terribly distracted. By sin, by life itself. The average Sunday *New York Times* now holds more information, front to back, than people in the nineteenth century typically learned over the course of their whole lives. Is it any wonder we're distracted? Overwhelmed? So lost on the surface we can't dig any deeper? Who has the time? Who has the energy?

It's precisely this insidious new craziness in our world that Satan loves to use against us. How better to keep us from the God who saves? It doesn't feel evil; it's just life, right? Or is it? When we finally remember *again* what life is all about, what is truly important and good and right and meaningful, and that we came screaming into the world naked and we're going to heaven without a U-Haul...then He welcomes us back with open arms. And our attention, our rededication of soul time with Him, is honored in ways we have yet to fully discover.

Come away, friend. Do not rush this! These prayers/stories are meant to be read one per sitting, and read slowly. Take some deep breaths. Detox. Call out to Him. *Enter into* these prayers. Become the narrator. Use them as metaphors for your own life. They are fictional, written only to inspire and help you come closer to what lies in the depths of your soul. But God can use them in astounding ways, like He can use anything—ask Him to show you more about Himself, more about you, through them. Use the imperative comments (set in italics and flush right) as places to make the prayers your own, unique to you and your situation. It is my hope that these prayers will serve as the springboard to inspire you to "see" Jesus beside you, regardless of where you live or what you go through, and that it will lead you to see Him beside you forevermore, in prayer, in day-to-day life. Throw away your doubts and open your heart to the Holy. To remember...remember...remember...

Foster writes, "Love is the response of the heart to the overwhelming goodness of God, so come in simply and speak to him in unvarnished honesty." Brennan Manning calls it "the wisdom of accepted tenderness." My hope is that *God Encounter* becomes one of the most primary, basic, moving paths on which we can experience an encounter with the Holy and discover what He's all about. My hope is that this book will awaken in us a whole new avenue toward a developing, deepening relationship with God. My hope is that it draws each of us closer to the Savior each time we meet Him on the road.

A word of caution. Our Lord God created our imagination and made us a creative people, but Satan can distort those faculties (Romans 1:21). This should not prohibit us from retaking this gift from the Enemy. But Foster urges us to "sanctify the imagination"—

> to seek God's thoughts after him, to delight in his presence, to desire his truth and his way. The more we live in this way, the more God utilizes our imagination for his good purposes. To believe God can sanctify and utilize the imagination is simply to take seriously the Christian idea of incarnation. God so accommodates, so enfleshes himself into our world, that he uses the images we know and understand to teach us about the unseen world of which we know so little and find so difficult to understand.

I've included a prayer that precedes each creative prayer, asking God to specifically protect us as we give our imaginations and hearts free reign to better understand Him.

Whereas Eastern traditions teach meditation in order that followers might empty themselves out—to essentially *lose* themselves—Christian meditation should be designed to bring us face to face with God in order that we might choose Him over ourselves, find Christ *within* us, hear what He has to say to us time and time again. We are called to repent, to modify our behavior, to desire to draw ever closer to this God above all gods, the Lord God on high. When we truly encounter the living God, we find that Jesus is standing alongside us, ready to heal, teach, forgive, and give us hope for our future.

Thomas Merton writes,

> Anyone who imagines he can simply begin
> meditating without praying for the desire
> and the grace to do so, will soon give up. But
> the desire to meditate, and the grace to begin
> meditating, should be taken as an implicit
> promise of further graces.

Begin there, my friend, and all the rest will come. In fact, you're probably there already, since you picked up this book. Keep your eyes on Jesus, and only good will follow.

LISA BERGREN

June 2002

Chapter One

❧

THE CABIN

WHEN YOU FEEL LOST, WEARY, AND AFRAID

God is our protector.

MATTHEW 11:28

Be still before the Lord: Take a deep, slow breath through your nostrils, filling your lower lungs first, then the middle of the lungs, then the top. Hold it for a moment, then release it slowly through your mouth. Repeat ten times.

Read and reflect: Read this scripture verse until you can repeat it three times without looking: "Come to me, all you who are weary and burdened, and I will give you rest" (Matthew 11:28).

Ask yourself how you're weary and burdened and how your heart longs for rest.

Enter into prayer: As you read through the cabin scene described in the following pages, pause periodically to focus on your senses, bringing the scene to life. Use the ends of paragraphs to pause and consider sight, smell, sound, and touch. Read each sentence slowly, pausing often to dwell on the meaning for you.

As you begin, take a deep, slow breath. In and out, in and out. And pray this prayer:

Lord, I hear Your invitation: "Come to me, all you who are weary and burdened, and I will give you rest." Father in heaven, help me to understand how I might seek You out and trust You with the load I carry. Remind me how You're ever present, and keep the devil away from my door, away from my heart. Sanctify my imagination, Lord. In Jesus' name. Amen.

I'M WALKING in the evening through a cool, dense forest. A squirrel comes down a ponderosa on my right to chatter a demand to leave his turf. A woodpecker ignores me, intent on finding a bug or making a home high on the pine above. To the west, a setting sun casts brilliant golds and oranges into the sky, visible in peekaboo views between the thick, green foliage.

On and on I walk. Ten minutes more. Twenty, spurred on by the peace and luxury of being alone.

> *Imagine yourself there, the soft give of the ground beneath your feet, the cool shadows upon your skin. See yourself at peace, enjoying the sense of exploration and solitude.*

The longer I walk, the more limber I feel. My legs feel longer, my arms swing easily at my sides. I breathe deeply to fully appreciate the odors of pine and pitch, of decomposing needles, of the moist loam of the forest floor. But I'm tiring.

*Imagine yourself thinking about returning home but longing
to stay where you are. It's enticing. Too perfect to ignore.*

I'm reluctant to turn back. The sunset is beautiful where
the trees open up just enough to observe it, a painting that
seems made just for me. Gradually it fades to watercolor
hues of pale yellow and washed-out peach, then the dim
glow and deep shadows of twilight. And I know it's best I
head home.

I turn around, intent on retracing my steps, and discover
that nothing looks familiar—my footprints have been covered by the knee-high ferns easily parted and just as easily
rejoined. I stifle a heart flutter of concern. I left the path just
over that hill, right?

I decide on a direction, feeling fairly confident that this is
the way. But I don't find the path over the hill or over the next.

After half an hour, I conclude that all is definitely not
right. After drinking the last drips from my water bottle, I
turn again.

*Pause for a moment to consider the sensation
of being lost. Remember what it felt like?
Or if you've never been lost, what it might feel like?*

This direction also proves to be wrong. How could I be
so lost? So fast? I retrace in my mind those landmarks I

remember seeing last along my original path, but nothing here is familiar. I orient myself to the last vestiges of the fading twilight, knowing the sun had been right there—*right there!*—and it makes sense to head in the opposite direction. Doesn't it? I'm confused, my thoughts tumbling about like clothes in a dryer.

Fear is rising in my mind as darkness continues to deepen, faster and faster. It suddenly seems like I've been walking for hours. My muscles ache, begging me to stop. My throat is raw from thirst. My stomach growls in frustration.

A crashing sound through the nearby brush sends me whirling, my heart pounding. It's just a deer, I tell myself, but I still turn on my heel and rush away.

On and on I go, ducking a tree branch here, stumbling over a root there. The branches whip my face; the thick underbrush pokes and scratches my legs. With each step I'm growing more tired and weary and frightened.

> *Feel the fear rising inside you,*
> *crowding your heart.*

It's dark now, completely dark. I can see a dim outline of a thick tree trunk to my left and reach out to steady myself, noting the spongy puzzle-piece texture of ponderosa bark and the stickiness of pitch. I pant from the exertion.

My heart pounds. My hands and face would be sweating

if I weren't so, so cold. A shiver runs from my neck down my back.

I'm lost.

Feel your heart pounding.

I turn west—what I think might be west—hoping to catch one last hint of twilight.

Nothing. All is darkness. In a slow circle I turn, widening my eyes to try to see better, wiping away the droplets of rain now falling and slipping down my face.

It's crazy. I've walked in these woods a hundred times. But it's true. I'm lost.

I tremble from fear, from weariness, from the falling temperature. I berate myself for failing. For not turning back when I first thought about it. For being so dumb as to get lost. For leaving the path. For ignoring the encroaching darkness. But it had been so nice out, so lovely and enticing...

I'm lost.

You can't bed down here, I tell myself. *You'll die of hypothermia before daybreak.*

"Lord God, I need help."

Silently whisper it to Him now.

I'm lost, so lost. And so tired.

Imagine yourself calling out to Him again, this time a little louder.

I suddenly wonder if I have the strength to stand another moment. From neck to knee my body cries out for rest. Still, I walk on, hoping beyond hope.

Feel the weariness and hear yourself crying out to Him with growing anxiety.

I notice my feet getting wet inside my boots. I hear rushing water all around me. Have I stumbled into a shallow creek bed, flowing full now from the rain? Is the entire forest floor flooding?

"Lord God, help me!"

Silently cry it out.

"Lord, God of heaven, I'm lost and I'm afraid and I'm so, so weary. Come to me. Help me! In Jesus' name!"

Hear His name upon your tongue, your cry heavenward.

Another crash sounds nearby along the forest floor, and I shrink in fear. But wait...What is that? Light? I'm torn between consternation—was it a lightning strike?—and attraction—could I be close to a cabin? Warmth? Sanctuary?

"Hello? Is there anyone there?"

"Hello," a deep, welcoming voice greets me. I'm startled how it surrounds me. "It is I." The light grows brighter, and I feel warmer just with His drawing near.

> *You are not alone. It is He. God. Jesus. Look upon His face.*
> *Tell Him about your fears, what you've been through.*
>
> *Does He embrace you? Offer a strong hand? Pick you up*
> *and carry you? You feel He could carry the whole world.*
>
> *Welcome what He offers: Sanctuary.*

He doesn't ask. Somehow I know He understands what's in my heart. But I can't move. I'm too tired. Just too tired. I'm shaking from head to toe, and the trembling is taking every last ounce of energy I have...

As I collapse, He picks me up in His arms and pushes through the forest, His footsteps sure, His stride long. I haven't been carried since I was a child, and I fight off the longing for sleep, my eyelids so heavy. He hurries along when my trembling continues, seeming to know the urgency of my need for shelter.

"It's all right," He whispers. "I am here."

> *Deep inside you begin to feel a bit of warmth.*
> *Your trembling diminishes and stops.*

About five minutes later we emerge at the edge of the forest—I'd been so close, and yet so lost! A cheery little log cabin stands before us. Yellow light streams from its windows, speaking of a fire long laid and lit. I want to weep with relief. What is it, two, three in the morning? My family and neighbors will be so worried!

> *Feel the surprise of relief wash over you.*
> *A burst of energy, your second wind, surges through you.*

"It will be all right," my Savior says with absolute confidence, setting me down. "I am here. This is where you will rest tonight." With a gentle hand upon my shoulder, He leads me toward the immaculate cabin. It's only about fifteen by fifteen feet across.

He opens the door, and the cabin is as welcoming inside as it had seemed from outdoors. My Friend motions to a small side room. I know I must get out of my cold, damp clothes and eagerly step inside. I strip of my wet, clinging sweater and jeans and pull on a robe that's hanging on a peg. A huge, luxurious robe of the softest cotton I've ever felt. Then thick socks. I appreciate the feel of dry, warm clothing at last.

I comb out my hair and hesitantly return to the front room.

"There's a table set before you," He invites, gesturing toward it, seeming to know how hungry I am. I try not to rush the table, try not to wolf down the bread, but I can still smell yeast in the air, and the soft crust melts in my mouth. I gulp down the wine, then a glass of water. More bread, more wine, more water. At last, I'm sated.

Take a moment to feel the pleasure of a full stomach.

He gestures toward an overstuffed recliner set before the fire. I sit there, and He covers me with a blanket and sets a steaming cup of tea in my hands.

"Thank You, Lord," I whisper, overcome by how He was so ready to come to my rescue. My Deliverer, my Savior, my Rock, my Master.

Thank Him silently now. See Him smile back into your eyes.

"Tomorrow," He says, "you'll see the path home. Tonight, stay here and rest. I will guard the door. Do not fear."

He stares at me a moment longer. "Rest," He repeats.

How can I do anything else? With a full stomach, a warm wrap, the dancing fire before me, and a guard such as He at the door, how can I do anything but give in to the overwhelming desire to let my leaden eyelids fall?

My second wind has definitely faded away. I haven't been this tired, this relaxed, this assured since...

Since when?

I hear Him step outside, and I notice by the silence that the rain has ceased. And I know, deep inside, that He'll remain close by. I feel utterly safe, ready to give in to slumber. My breathing slows.

Breathe in...breathe out.

I will my eyes partially open to set down my teacup on the table beside me, and I glance again at the flames. Light dances around the dark walls, the flames themselves alternately scarlet and pumpkin and sapphire in color. It's entrancing.

I've never felt this peace, this security. Never. My breathing further slows and becomes even more rhythmic.

"Thank you, Father," I whisper.

Give Him thanks now.

I'm warm, I'm safe, and tomorrow I'll be home. "Rest," He said. No, He commanded it: "Rest."

Pause in silence for several breaths, considering what it means to come to Him, to give up your heavy burdens and worries and simply BE, resting in Him.

Amen.

Chapter Two

THE BAY

WHEN IT'S TIME TO RENEW YOUR PERSPECTIVE

God is good.

PSALM 34

Be still before the Lord: Slowly let your head drop to your chest and your spine curl forward. Feel the weight of your head and shoulders as they slump forward, and take note of the curve of your upper back. This should be a gentle stretch from your waist, all along your spine, through your neck.

Pause for a moment and breathe, stretching as long as you care to. You're letting your upper body give in to gravity, and it's working on the tension and aches in your shoulders, neck, and back.

Very, very slowly, come back to an erect posture, lifting your chin and pulling back your shoulders. Pay attention to the sensations coursing through you. Take several long, deep breaths, filling your lungs to capacity, pausing, then completely exhaling.

Read and reflect: God understands our feelings of being far from Him. Hear the words of the psalmist in these verses:

> My God, my God, why have you forsaken me?
> Why are you so far from saving me,
> so far from the words of my groaning?

O my God, I cry out by day, but you
do not answer,
by night, and am not silent.
(Psalm 22:1-2)

Have you ever felt this way? Far from Him? Finding it hard to concentrate on His goodness? His presence? He accepts that we have these feelings. But He also calls us back to recognition, to remembrance of the goodness of His very nature.

Hear these words too:

Great is the LORD and most worthy
of praise;
his greatness no one can fathom.
One generation will commend your works
to another....
They will tell of the power of your
awesome works,
and I will proclaim your great deeds.
They will celebrate your abundant goodness
and joyfully sing of your righteousness.
(Psalm 145:3-7)

Take a couple of minutes to contemplate what keeps you from the God of love and what reminds you of that love.

Enter into prayer: Pause periodically to focus on your senses, bringing the scene described below to life. Use the ends of paragraphs to stop and consider sight, smell, sound, and touch. Read each sentence slowly, pausing often to dwell upon the meaning for you.

Take a deep, slow breath. In and out, in and out. Lift up to God this prayer:

You are great, Lord, and most worthy of praise. Help me see Your awesome works in my life, and I will celebrate them and thank You. As I consider when and where I'm missing Your goodness in my life, keep evil thoughts far from me. Amen.

IT'S A FOGGY DAY, and in the distance I hear the lonely horn of a barge. I'm about to begin my day as I've begun a thousand days before it—sculling, rowing across the quiet waters of the bay.

It's uncommonly quiet out this morning, I notice, with few boats—or few foghorns anyway. The water is unusually calm beneath thick clouds of mist. It's as if the world has taken a day off. Perhaps this day won't be spent dodging tankers and sailboats and pleasure cruisers. Perhaps this day I can find a few moments of silence and peace. My life has been spinning lately, my heart as shrouded as the early morning sky around me.

*Imagine yourself there, having settled into one of the long boats
used by serious rowers, about to work out, in both body
and mind. What plagues you? What is unsettled inside you?
Why? Do you feel distant from God?*

Eagerly I grip the long, elegant oars and take a deep breath of moist, briny air.

I bend forward, feeling the gentle stretch of spine and neck and shoulder, anticipating the moment when I'll glide through the water as easily as a porpoise. The oars dip, plunge, and I pull...bend...pull...bend...pull...smiling as I pick up speed.

*Feel yourself bending, pulling, feeling the stretch
through your arms and shoulders and back.*

I head toward the bridge, which I can't yet see. Soon it emerges, monstrous and red from the foggy bank of morning, like a sea monster peeking up from the depths. It is mysterious and mesmerizing, especially on somber, silent days like this one.

The muscles in my shoulders and upper back tense, then gradually loosen as they warm to the exercise. My stomach tightens in response to the needs of my back. I'm flying, flying across the water.

With each pull, I pray. "Lord God, where are You?"

Bend...pull...

"Father God, come to me."

Bend...pull...

"Heavenly Father, I feel far from You."

Bend...pull...

With each pull, I pour out my complaints to Him. Everything that's wrong in my life. About my family, my friends, my work, my body, my church...everything.

Silently pour out your complaints now.

Bend...pull...bend...pull...bend...pull...

I row across the water until my prayer of complaint is complete, until my arms and shoulders scream for release, until I reach the bridge.

I look up to the top, impossibly high, making me wonder at the courage of the men who built her. She seems to soar, this bridge, to have a life of her own.

Other than the shallow waves, it's utterly peaceful, a sensation I've never, ever experienced on such a busy bay. Usually the water is sea-sloppy or wind-rough. Today, the water laps against my boat, and I pant from the exertion, but otherwise, there's no other sound—except for the muffled commuter car engines humming across the bridge and the broken, rhythmic sound of wheels crossing the section dividers. It's a ghostly song, from far away it seems, even though it's almost directly above.

I turn my attention back to God. Back to the cry in my heart. "Lord, come to me. Come to me, please. I need You here. I need You close."

Gradually, I become aware of His presence, like the sticky air that clings to every pore of my skin. He has heard my call. It surprises me, His speed. His willingness to come. Right here. To me, of all people.

Pause to contemplate His presence now. What does it feel like?

In His presence, I'm reminded of His goodness. His willingness to draw near to me at the asking. His abiding Spirit ready to sit with me, right here in this boat.

All at once, all the good things in my life flood through my mind. Every good thing about my family and friends and work and body and church...everything.

Give Him thanks for every good thing you can think of now.

"My good and gracious God, you've been so generous to me," I pray. All of a sudden, everything is seen from a new perspective.

My knee aches on damp days like this, but I have the strength to go rowing every morning. Things haven't been the best with my friend lately, but I have many friends, and I have the means to make things right with the one friend who has been bothering me. My pastor has been less than inspirational lately, but I have the freedom to worship and commune with fellow believers, when elsewhere in the world, doing so would send me to prison.

Put each of your complaints into the perspective of greater vision.

Gradually, just as the bridge emerges from under her gray veil, so does my heart. The sun pierces the damp cloth that covers the city, splitting it apart and gently easing it away. The more I think about all God has done in my life, the more my heart sings of His goodness.

I can't believe I've ever had a complaint. How could I when I remember all that's right and happy and good in my life?

Consider, for a moment, what it feels like when you have a radical change of heart, of understanding. Feel God's light enter you, pushing away the darkness.

"Lord God, forgive me for my forgetfulness. I have spiritual amnesia. Help me to always remember Your graciousness and to forget my meddlesome troubles. Give me Your focus, Your vision, that I might better reflect Your light. Make me a lighthouse, Lord, and You the lamp. Amen."

The sun completes its work, and the fog is at last in full retreat toward the expansive ocean, a great, billowing, swirling cloud of silver. Had I been lost in its darkness? I feel the heat of the morning sun on my scalp and smile.

"Amen," I repeat, as if in benediction, resolving to remember His goodness in the midst of any strife. To remember.

Remember.

Remember.

I reach forward and pull to return to the dock.

Bend forward...pull...

Amen...

Bend...pull...

Amen...

Bend...pull...

Amen. ✎

Chapter Three

❧

HOLY OF HOLIES

WHEN YOU YEARN FOR SOMEONE
GREATER THAN YOURSELF

God is holy.

PSALM 96:4-9

Be still before the Lord: Fast breathing can wake you up and clear your head. For ten seconds, breathe rapidly in and out through your nose, with your mouth closed. Take a long, deep, slow breath. Then breathe rapidly in and out for twenty seconds. Finish with one long, deep breath, feeling the chest expand outward in all directions, normal exhalation, then another long, deep breath with very slow exhalation, until you feel your chest deflate. Return to normal, quiet breathing.

Read and reflect: Read these words from Psalm 96:4-9:

> For great is the LORD and most worthy
>   of praise;
>   he is to be feared above all gods.
> For all the gods of the nations are idols,
>   but the LORD made the heavens.
> Splendor and majesty are before him;
>   strength and glory are in his sanctuary.
> Ascribe to the LORD, O families of nations,
>   ascribe to the LORD glory and strength.

Ascribe to the LORD the glory due his name;
    bring an offering and come into his courts.
Worship the LORD in the splendor
        of his holiness;
    tremble before him, all the earth.

Now read them again, pausing after each phrase to take in the meaning of the words.

Read them a third time, considering what it would mean to come face to face with the living God.

On the fourth time, make the psalm a prayer to Him: *You are great, Lord, and worthy of praise, to be feared above all gods. For all gods of the nations are idols, but You made the heavens! Splendor and majesty are before You; strength and glory are in Your sanctuary. I glorify You, honor You, because You are worthy; I bring You the offering of myself as I come into Your court. I worship You. I tremble before You. You are holy. You are my Lord God Almighty. Thank you for calling me here. Amen.*

Enter into prayer: Pause periodically to focus on your senses, bringing the following scene to life. Use the ends of paragraphs to stop and consider sight, smell, sound, and touch. Read each sentence slowly, pausing often to dwell upon the meaning for you.

Lord God, sanctify my imagination and keep the Evil One far from me. Please use this prayer to help me catch a glimpse of the wonder and glory of Your holiness. Help me to dare to sense a part of You inside of me, longing to commune with You, outside of me. In Jesus' name. Amen.

Take a deep, slow breath. In and out, in and out.

I glorify and honor You, Lord, because You're worthy; I bring You the offering of myself as I come into Your court. I worship You. I tremble before You. You are holy. You are my Lord God Almighty. Thank You for calling me here.

I'VE BEEN ON THE PATH for some time. My throat is as dry and dusty as the dirt beneath my feet. I try to gather enough saliva in my mouth to make a difference, but to no avail. The arid countryside is strewn with rocks, reminding me of the border country of a high desert.

I pause. When will I arrive?

There it is again, on the wind—the faintest whisper of my name on the breeze. Again!

My name, twice. I'm sure of it. Who's calling me? Am I so dehydrated that I'm hallucinating?

> *Pause for a moment to consider what it would sound like,*
> *hearing your name on the wind.*

It's a hot day, probably hovering around ninety, but it's a dry heat. I look down to see the remnants of my sandals barely holding on and find it difficult to care. I wear a tunic of white, or what was once white, and am grateful for its light weight.

On and on I walk, uphill, into the wind that bears my name.

I crest a small knoll and discover a bright, shining city on the gently sloping mountain before me. At the top of a monstrous city wall is a temple. The gold on its roof makes me squint as it reflects the harsh summer sun. What is this place? And why is there no one else around?

I hear my name again, this time like a faint whisper from across a deserted sanctuary. I'm getting closer. Licking my dry, parched lips, I move forward again.

The closer I get to the ancient city, the more apprehensive I become. The dry bones of the dead are strewn here and there among decapitated statues of gods and goddesses, idols of old, as if they reached this place at last, then gave in to death.

I pause, considering the idols in my own life. Inherently I understand that idols take different shapes, that this graveyard is a graphic lesson for me. For me alone. The idols gradually take on the shape of my own sins. Ambition, greed, envy, laziness...

Silently name your idols now. Things that keep you from the Holy One. From the temple.

The sound of my name is clearer now, each syllable clearly enunciated. I gaze back toward the shining city and begin walking again, a feeling of dread and fear suddenly stealing across my heart. But I can do nothing else. There's no one to ask about this voice calling to me, no one to ask why I'm here all alone.

Deep within, I sense some recognition, but I shove the knowledge away, afraid. All I know is that I must go on.

To my right is a sloping hill covered with the silver green of olive trees. To my left are the remains of an old city, all a jaundiced tan, the color of limestone. Where are the people? I suddenly long for human contact, anyone to consult on this mad escapade into a deserted—is it deserted?—temple. Someone to join me, keep me from these feelings of vulnerability, of fear.

I hear my name again, this time as loud as a stage whisper from ten feet away.

Hear your name now.

"Hello?"

But only silence greets me.

Wide steps—ancient steps—disappear under two great, curved archways, along with the stark, harsh light of the outdoors. I take a few hesitant steps upward. "Hello?"

My attention is turned to the scent of something unmistakable. Water.

> *Take a deep breath and imagine the smell, after a long, dry, dusty road. Does it smell of river and reeds and...life?*

I turn and spy two wide, still, deep pools on either side of the stairs, and the cry that leaves my throat is something animal, primal in nature, but I don't care. All I care about is the water.

I rush down to one of them, stumbling, righting myself, pushing onward. Madly, I cup my hands and fill my mouth, covering my face, but it isn't enough. I'm so thirsty that even my bones seem as dry as those I passed along the road.

I drink and drink, amazed at the sweetness rolling over my tongue—like the best well water in the world, the most expensive bottled import—better than anything I've ever tasted.

The thirst in my throat is thoroughly assuaged, but I dunk my whole face in, still longing for more—for immersion, cleansing, enough water to sate my thirst from the *inside out*. And I long to rid myself of the dust that covers me from grimy hair root to filthy toenail.

Then, beneath the pool's surface, I see steps leading forward. Without further hesitation I clamber down the stairs, slipping into the waters.

I cry out in ecstasy at the sensation, pure wonder in being covered, surrounded, enveloped in deliciously refreshing liquid. It's as if I've never experienced a bath or a swim before. But it *is* unlike anything I've ever experienced.

Scrubbing down my body, washing away the dust that has plagued me from the long, wearisome road, I move to my feet and scrape the mud from under my nails. I wash the back of my neck and the inside of my ears, relishing the feel of being clean at last.

See yourself cleaning your dust-covered skin, cleansing your body from head to heel. Feel your body cool in the perfect temperature of the water.

When I'm finished with my bath, I float on my back. For the first time all day, I don't resist the sun beating down upon me. With my ears underwater, the few sounds are muted— an occasional *swoosh* from my hand or a gentle kick of my feet to keep myself afloat.

Remember a time you floated on your back, the sensation of being nearly weightless, the muffled underwater sounds.

I remain there until the sound of my name enters my ears—not like the garbled sounds of someone above water, speaking to me through the depths—but as clear as a secret shared between friends.

What would that sound be like?

I right myself quickly, gazing about, but there's nobody with me.

"Hello?"

My fear turns to irritation and anger. Who's playing with me? I step out of the water and rush up the stairs beside the pool. The answer, I'm sure, is ahead.

The steps emerge under a colonnade that opens to a mammoth courtyard. Before me, at last, is the temple. In the depths of my heart, I know that it's here I've been called.

Hesitantly, I run a hand over my water-slicked hair and glance down at my tunic, quickly drying in the parched air. Instinctively, I bend to remove my old, decrepit sandals—it seems disrespectful to enter a holy place in shoes such as these. I walk barefoot across the cobblestones to the wide entrance of the temple.

Fifteen-foot-wide doors of paneled cypress are open, as if beckoning to me.

A wave of sound washes through me, like the time I heard a choir sing as a single perfect voice lifted to heaven. The wave sends a shiver from the nape of my neck to the small of my back, then another down my shoulders.

Consider a sound such as this. What is your reaction?

The rough hand-hewn stones transition to smooth marble beneath my feet. I look around and up, higher still, and gasp. The room must be sixty feet long, thirty feet wide, and forty-five feet high, with windows on both sides. How could I be the only one in this lovely place? this holy sanctuary? Why is it not filled with worshipers?

I enter in, lips slightly apart in wonder and awe. Muted light streams in from the windows, leaving shadowy, slanting columns of dancing dust before me. The walls are covered in carved cedar wood, depicting plants and flowers. I gasp again when I realize that my toes touch not marble but gold.

The sound of my name comes again, this time from beyond an altar that smells of old incense. As I pass it, I hear a song that seems to come from nearby. The song is like a Latin hymn of adoration sung by a men's choir, and they sing with such sincere reverence it sends another shiver down my back.

When the song is ended, a deep, royal voice calls to me again, this time in the tone of a king to his subject.

I dare not ask who He is. I know.

Who is it? Who's your King?
What would He sound like in this place?

Could this be happening? To me? I'm just a normal person from a normal town who lives in a normal house...

He says my name again, and I scurry forward, through a massive thirty-foot-long curtain of heavy woven yarn—blue, purple, and scarlet. And it has been torn down the middle—which seems impossible when I realize the curtain's density and thickness. But it allows entry to this place, and I'm glad for it.

Almost glad. A curious mix of intense joy...and fear.

The floor and walls of this inner sanctum are covered with gold. Before me a flame burns five feet high but seems to have no source. I pause, casting about in my mind for the next logical step. But none of this is logical.

"L-Lord?"

Hear yourself say His name now.

In tandem with my call, the flame flickers and dances before me like what I imagine Moses saw in the burning bush. My eyes widen. My senses are on heightened alert. My pulse pounds in my ears.

The Holy of Holies.

I have a personal audience with the Lord God.

The God of Abraham and Isaac and Jacob.

The God above all gods. My God. With me. Alone.

"I shouldn't be here, Lord," I whisper, shaking my head, slowly backing away. "I'm so unworthy. I'm so—"

My name on His tongue stops my speech, and this time the sound of it reverberates through my chest like the deep bass of a concert loudspeaker.

Hear it now; feel it in your chest.

Overwhelmed, shocked by the force of it, I fall to my knees, then to my face before Him. The cool, gold flooring meets my feverish face. The phrase *fear of the Lord* suddenly makes instant sense to me.

But after a frightening pause, His voice surrounds me like the loving arms of a father reaching for a hurt child, and I dare to take a breath. He whispers my name, coaxing, persuading, confirming.

The sound of my name on the wind.

I may rise to my knees and look upon Him. I know this.

I get to my knees but cannot summon the courage to look again. I fear that gazing upon one square inch of Him might send my heart into overload; it's already pounding at a crazy rate. Trembling overtakes my body, as if I'm cold. I glance at my hands.

It is fear that causes me to shake. Wonder. Respect. Awe of His holy power.

But I'm drawn to Him, undeniably transfixed by this inexplicable, overwhelming, holy experience. At the same time I want to escape from here, I also yearn for this experience never to end.

He lifts my chin, inviting me to know Him. And His touch floods me with warmth, with understanding. Tenderness.

Hear what He has to tell you.

About your misery and shame.

About forgiveness.

About the promises He has for you.

"But Lord, why me? Why call me here?"

"So that you might know I AM," He says.

Another phrase I've puzzled over. I AM. I silently repeat His name—I AM, I AM, I AM—mulling it over.

Consider God's name for a moment.
What does it mean for Him to be I AM?

And then it hits me.

He *is*. He is! He is everything! No beginning, no end. The Eternal! Right here!

Right here.

Love and glory and peace and joy flood my heart in a mad, tumbling rush.

"O Lord, thank You for bringing me here. You are holy! You are righteous! And You are my King! I worship You."

I fall to my face again.

And His blessing surrounds me like a welcome cloak of honor.

Feel it nestle about you like a warm, welcome, soft blanket.

But it isn't over. As you sit before Him, entirely
anchored in the presence of the Holy, you find a new
level of communion with Him through silence.

*How do you understand this communion? Sense it? Consider
for a moment this deeper level of understanding, this connection
that doesn't rely on speech but on knowing. Feel it enter you,
surround you, piercing your heart and shining through the other side.
It is beyond words, so much better than you can describe, isn't it?*

The air quietly fills with the high-pitched echoing sound
of a boys' choir; I cannot make out the words but long to
join in.

"You are holy, Lord!" I shout. "The Most High! Thank
You for showing me this place! I never knew You were here!
I would have come before, had I known."

*Praise Him now, hearing the holy music. Praise His holiness,
His willingness to call you forward. Praise Him as the God on high.*

I cannot stop the praises that keep coming from my
heart as the unseen choir quietly crescendos in the highest,
clearest, sweetest, prettiest notes I've ever heard. I can't
believe I was so close to this place and yet so distant.

"Precious child of mine," He says, "I was here all along.
And I will be with you for all eternity."

Amen. ✄

Chapter Four

FROM A WHEAT FIELD
TO AN ASPEN GROVE

WHEN YOU NEED GUIDANCE

God is our guide.

PSALM 48:14

Be still before the Lord: This is called "invisible motion." Find a comfortable seat with your feet firmly planted on the ground before you. Place your hands on your legs. Close your eyes and take three deep breaths. In...and out. In...out. In...out.

Now make the tiniest motion of your head you can perceive, whether from left to right or up and down. Let your senses inform you of this tiny movement. Concentrate on how your body responds. Take a deep breath as you continue this practice.

While keeping your eyes closed and focused on the tiny movements you're making with your head, imagine that you're slowly approaching a much-sought-after prize, like a lion on the prowl, hunting. Any sudden movement will send the prey flying away. Keep your motions still and quiet.

Read and reflect: As you see yourself creeping ever closer, listen to this scripture from Daniel:

> Praise be to the name of God for ever and ever;
> wisdom and power are his.

He changes times and seasons;
> he sets up kings and deposes them.
He gives wisdom to the wise
> and knowledge to the discerning.
He reveals deep and hidden things;
> he knows what lies in darkness,
> and light dwells with him. (2:20-22)

Think about what remains dark to you, what you seek His light and guidance on. Name it. See it as a small round object lying just before you, the thing you're hunting. Imagine yourself edging closer and closer with your quiet, subtle movements until you lean down—slowly, ever so slowly—until you can gently scoop it up and hold it in your hands.

Now see yourself grinning as a light comes through the darkness, and you suddenly view your problem or puzzle in a different way. Hold on to the hint of that revelation as you enter into this next prayer.

And listen again to these words from the passage in Daniel: *He reveals deep and hidden things; he knows what lies in darkness.*

Enter into prayer: As you read through the following scene, place yourself in the position of the narrator. Don't let details trip you up; simply move forward and see yourself in his or her place. Pause periodically to focus on your senses, bringing the scene to life. Use the ends of paragraphs to stop and consider sight, smell, sound, and touch. Read each sentence slowly, pausing often to dwell upon the meaning for you.

Take a deep, slow breath. In and out, in and out. Pray this prayer of protection:

Lord God, as I begin to pray, help me to see where You want to lead me, to teach me. Help me to be open to Your way. Show me how to take the next step. Keep the powers of darkness away and fill me only with Your light. In Jesus' name. Amen.

I PULL OFF the hot, dusty gravel road into a familiar, shallow turnoff. Shifting the old Ford into park, I turn the key and the truck shudders to a stop. I shove open the creaking door and slide to the ground; a puff of dust rises around my sneakers. It's quiet here, on the edge of the wheat field, a constant, silent invitation every time I pass by.

Slamming the door shut, I take a long look in both directions of this seldom-traveled farm road. No one else within reach of sight or sound.

Moving to the wire gate, I pull up on the rusted latch and step through, carefully shutting it behind me. The owner of this farm is an old friend. I'm a welcome guest, not a trespasser, and I treat everything with studious respect, wanting to preserve my status.

I begin walking up a slight hill, through wheat the color just beyond summer yellow and well on its way to autumn gold. Cresting the small hill, slightly out of breath, I gaze across acres and acres of a harvest-to-be, smiling for what must be the first time today, after a long day of work.

This, this is where I find it. When I'm feeling lost and unsure and wondering if I'll ever find my path again. This is where He meets me.

Across about five acres of wheat is a forested hill. Beyond it towers the blue-green of the mountains. The evening light illuminates the bottoms of the mountains in the near distance, making them more obviously forested, creating shadows behind each tree, giving them a velvety texture I want to reach out and touch.

There's no place like this mountain valley, verdant in her belly, promising with each peak. I take a slow 360-degree turn, feeling cradled in the valley's arms. Feeling cradled in *His* arms for the first time all day, all week, all month...

> *Take a moment to see yourself there. Focus on all you can see, smell, hear, feel. Deep breath in...and out. In...and out.*

A slow smile spreads across my face, and I again set off across the field. "Lord God," I whisper, "come to me now. Join me here. Let me feel Your presence. Please."

Hear your silent, whispered plea now.

"Lord God, Jesus, I've been sinful and away from You. Please cleanse my heart and soul and help me to commit more and more of myself to You each day."

Silently hear your own confession.

Striding through the waist-high wheat stalks, my senses are on heightened alert. I'm ready for this meeting with God. Almost. "Forgive me my unbelief, Father. Help me to believe. You can meet me here. You can see me through this. You see me through anything. I need you. Come to me now."

Silently invite Him closer.

I walk and pray, walk and pray, feeling the stress of the day ease out of my neck...and shoulders...and out through my fingertips as I walk.

Feel that stress leaving your neck and shoulders, down your arms and out through your fingertips. Deep breathe in...and out. See yourself walking, inviting God to come closer in a tangible way.

The slope becomes steep again. My fingers brush through the straw stalks, the stiff kernels of wheat, the wiry tendrils on each head. I close my eyes, inhaling the scent of this rich farmland I've always known, a scent mingled with a hint of pine from the nearing hillside. I'm almost there.

"Come to me, Lord. Walk with me, Jesus. Please."

See yourself walking with eyes closed, confident with each step, your hand reaching out from your body along the tops of the wheat.

I grin. I reach again and then smile some more. Another's hand. I open my eyes and smile at Jesus, walking alongside me.

Does He reach for your hand and take it firmly in His own? What does that feel like? Imagine Him silent for the moment, communicating only in action. How do you feel in His presence? Excited? All senses on alert? Awed? Thankful? For a moment, consider all you're sensing now.

He speaks for the first time. My name is the first thing He says.

Hear how He says it. It sounds different from how others speak it. Your name. Hear it now in your heart.

He knows why I've invited Him near. He always knows before a word of it leaves my lips, but I feel compelled to say the reason aloud. This thing, this idea, this problem has been plaguing me for days or weeks or months or years. "I know

You know this, Lord, but I'm confused and need Your guidance. Can You show me...?"

Continue on, silently telling Him the ways
in which you need His guidance.

He smiles in reassurance and takes the lead. I pass from the wheat field and out onto the rocks of the granite hillside, strewn with ponderosa and tamarack. He gives me a hand up onto the first boulder, then the next, over a wide chasm and onward, up the hill. Hand in hand with my Savior, I have no fear, just wonder, awe. I've been here before, know what's coming, but I need this. Over and over, I need this.

The spring has been here for centuries, the headwaters to a creek that contributes to a mighty river that feeds the valley and waters her crops and supplies life to her people. I take a deep breath, inhaling new smells of damp peat and of water pooling in tiny dips of rock.

The sun is fading. My Friend, my Counselor leads me to a grove of aspen that lines the quiet stream, the leaves set to dancing in the slight breeze that rustles my hair.

Feel the anticipation run through your body, from scalp to toe.

In front of me, He ducks and pulls back a branch, then another, opening the way for me. When I reach the center of perhaps fifty aspen—some as old as thirty or forty years—I settle onto nature's bed of fallen leaves and twigs and grasses.

Beside me, the creek babbles and dances over mossy rocks, creating miniature waterfalls as it makes its way ever onward. My Counselor kneels before me, then reaches toward the silver-blue water. He dips in His hand, deep, almost to the bottom, then brings it back up, His hand cupping the liquid that trickles down the side and off His wrist. It reflects the dusky sunlight and sky and trees around me, and I cannot take my eyes from it. Until He again speaks my name.

Hear your name on His tongue again, then...

"Remember the waters of your baptism," He says. "You are mine. Never far. I am always near." He kneels before me. With a wet fingertip, He traces the sign of the cross on my forehead as I close my eyes. He takes my hands in His.

Feel the cooling air on the damp shape of the cross on your forehead...
and the warmth of His big, dry hands holding your own.

"I'm forgetful, Lord. Forgive me. Help me in my unbelief."

Silently confess what holds you back.

But He knows. He already knows everything about me.

Yet as I talk and talk and talk, my burden lightens. I feel it ease from my shoulders...and down my arms...out through my fingertips and into His hands. He's taking it from me, assuming my burden.

Is it a burden that never should have been mine?

"I'm foolish, Savior. Grabby. Willing to assume too much, unwilling to believe enough. Forgive me. I know You're always with me. I want to trust, to believe. But I forget, and I get distracted, and..."

Tell Him all that's in your heart. Look into His eyes. What is there? Understanding? Gentle amusement? Peace? Fasten onto the sense of peace emanating from Him, entering you. Concentrate on that peace and reassurance. Deep breathe in...and out.

I remember that He speaks to me all the time, not just in this special place among the aspen, but also in a quiet look from a stranger, through a word from a friend, by a nudge in my heart... In countless ways He speaks to me every day. If I pay attention.

"I will lead you if you choose to follow," He says. "This burden that worries you will be resolved in time. You will mount up on eagle's wings. You will walk and not grow faint. Trust Me. *Believe.* All will be worked out in time. You will see."

He nods at the creek.

What does He tell you about the headwaters? The creek that nourishes the river that feeds the whole valley? Take a moment to listen.

I close my eyes and remember the feel of His fingertip tracing cool water lines on my forehead. The sign of the cross. The reminder of the baptism that made me His. He's never far. I am the one who strays from His side.

He rises now, quietly departing, but I sense He's still here. I'm not sad or bereft but comforted, at peace.

Deep breathe in...and out. He will see you through this.

Deep breathe in...and out. He'll show you the way.

Deep breathe in...and out. And you'll grow in better understanding of how He speaks to you.

I will follow His lead through big leaps and teeny, tiny, barely perceptible movements. And I'll give Him thanks for the patience He grants me in the meantime.

Silently praise Him for drawing close when you invite Him to do so, for drawing close when you're not even aware of it.

As you praise Him, pay attention to your stance.
In your creative prayer, do you remain seated? Do you bow? Do you stretch out your arms to the heavens?
Praise His name in every way you know how.

After a moment, I open my eyes and watch the green-gold leaves of aspen dance in the breeze. I tune in to the sounds of the creek beside me. I smile upward, knowing it will all come together for me, that this struggle, any struggle—mental, emotional, or physical—will be resolved in time. His time.

"Thank You, Father. Thank You."

Amen. ✒

Chapter Five

A DESERT RIDGE AND
SANDSTONE CANYONS

WHEN YOU LONG TO FEEL HIS PRESENCE

God is near.

PSALM 145:18

Be still before the Lord: Sometimes we just need a conscious nap. What does this mean? You can rest your head on your arms, on your desk, or lie flat. Close your eyes and *pretend* to nap. You might begin to drift off; most likely you'll just relax with some deep, soothing breathing.

Concentrate on this for five minutes, breathing slowly in through your nose, then out through your mouth, in through your nose, and out through your mouth...

Reflect: Focus on one of these things that the Holy Spirit can bring you: *calm, centeredness,* or *inspiration*—whichever quality you feel you need most today. Pay attention to the deep inner need for that quality in your life right now, right here.

As you breathe in slowly, focus on that quality—calm, centeredness, inspiration—picturing yourself becalmed, centered on Christ, or newly inspired. What does your face look like? Your shoulders? Your chest? Breathe in...breathe out.

Enter into prayer: Pause periodically to focus on your senses, bringing the desert scene described on the following pages to life. Use the ends of paragraphs to stop and consider sight, smell, sound, and touch. Read each sentence slowly, pausing often to dwell upon the meaning for you.

Take a deep, slow breath. In and out, in and out.

Father God, I enter here asking You to show me Your way and Your way only. I need You. I want You. Come to me now that I might know You better, feel You beside me. Keep the powers of darkness away from me. Help me to see You, Lord. Amen.

I STAND AT THE EDGE of a desert, a dry wind at my back, pausing before a monolithic cliff painted in colors of salmon and brick that towers perhaps three hundred feet above me. The breeze pushes my hair into my eyes, and I impatiently brush it away. I search the sandstone face before me, seeking the nearby fissure. The entrance to the canyon I want is hidden, difficult to find in the sea of masquerading rock. I've passed many canyons already, canyons with names like Escalante and Coyote, Hurricane Hollow and Davis Gulch. They are not the one I seek.

The faint sound of water brings my head to the right—north—and I begin walking again over a sand dune. My feet crush through the crusty surface and sink as my weight comes down on one foot, then the other. It's like treading in a bin of flour.

I finally reach the top, cresting the dune, and see the

remnant of a stream spreading out, then disappearing into the arid desert to my right. Waves of heat rising from the desert floor make the horizon appear out of focus.

> *See the serpentine water, blue on beige, disappearing into the desert flats. Feel the hot desert sun penetrating your skin.*

My attention returns to the flaming Navajo sandstone cliffs and the curving entrance from which the stream departs. This is the one. This is the canyon. I rush toward it and plunge inward, relieved to be out of the hot wind and in the shade. Here I have shelter, and the temperature comes down at least fifteen degrees.

> *Take a moment to pause, sensing the relief of the shade from the desert heat, of the dry breeze around you, the remote, utter loneliness of this place. Deep breathe in...and out.*

I've been told by a colleague that this canyon path has brought her uncommon peace and direction. A mysterious thing to say, for sure, but intriguing, and I haven't been able to get her words out of my mind ever since. With one more touch to the half-empty canteen at my waist and the hand-drawn map in my sweaty fist, I move inward, listening to the haunting sound of wind at the mouth of the cavern, a far-off foghorn of sorts. It alternately sounds like a child with an old whistle, unable to get a tight seal, and like my grandfather's blowing on the edge of a bottle.

Imagine yourself there, stepping on damp sand.
Hear the wind. The hollow, muted sound of it.

Thousands of years of water, frost, and wind have hewn this curvy pathway through the ancient sandstone, exposing layers of rock that would delight geologists. The colors are a marvel—adobe and sand and suede—a hundred desert hues that could only be painted by the Creator's hand. Here and there, scrub brush or prickly pear emerge, but the foliage is sparse.

At times the stream flows to ankle depth, but hiking boots keep my feet dry. I plow through with little concern. Occasionally the stream widens to a damp, seeping, barely-moving presence on the sandy floor.

I edge left, then right, then left again. My friend said I would travel long but not get far along this sacred path. I've traveled over a mile in my twisted course but have probably only moved a couple hundred feet into this canyon, as a bird would fly above it. I continue on, hoping it will ultimately lead me to what I seek: An audience with my King.

Consider for a moment what an audience
with the Holy One might be like.

The wind picks up suddenly, roaring toward me. I turn instinctively toward it, as if facing an oncoming tidal wave.

Grit pelts my face, and I close my eyes and quickly turn away, trying to find a spot where I can breathe.

Hold your breath as if you're there. Then take shallow breaths.

The wind howls down and all around like a wolf bent on devouring me. "Lord, please," I pray. "Please!" Blinded, desperate for sanctuary, I feel along the coarse, sandpapery texture of the walls for an indentation big enough to slip into—somewhere, anywhere I can catch my breath and see. Momentary blindness sends a wave of panic through me.

"Please," I repeat in petition, "I'm here to seek You. In Jesus' name, help me!"

Silently repeat your petition for help.

Still blinded, I wince as my fingers meet a sharp edge. I pull my hand to my lips and taste the copper of my own blood. "Father, please help me! Do You hear me?"

I pray again and again, calling out to Him, moving onward, still feeling the sand pelt my scalp and hearing it pepper my backpack. "Give me the faith, Lord. Give me the faith. I want to believe. I want to!"

There. At last. The wall rolls outward and suddenly dips inward. I plunge forward. For the first time in several minutes, I take a free breath of air unencumbered by sand.

Deep breathe in...and out...

I flush my eyes with the rest of the canteen water, anxious to see again. When the last trickle meets my face, I realize what I've done and desperately lick my fingers. There are occasional pools of rainwater along the way, but no guarantee that one is within reach, or safe to drink.

"Okay, Lord," I whisper. "You got me this far—You brought me here. Please see me through." Swallowing my fear in a what-feels-like-crazy decision to trust, I open my eyes and blink until I can see clearly. The howling wind has died as suddenly as it began, as if sucked out of the crevice by the giant mouth of God.

"Thank You," I breathe, surprise rendering me almost mute.

Thank Him silently.

How does He respond? Hear it now.

Can you hear His call to you? To move forward? He's beckoning.
What does it sound like? What does He say?

Obediently, I move back into the cavern pathway, looking for a moment in the direction from which I came. My eyes briefly rest on the boot tracks in the sand, fading as if washed by waves on a beach, not by the grit-laden wind. A thought springs to mind: *It would be wiser to go that way. To go home. While I still can.*

My ears strain to hear any warning of another sandstorm building down the way, at the mouth of the cavern. I feel like a rabbit afraid to leave the sanctuary of his shallow hole. I pause, but all I hear is my own pulse in my ears, blood pushing past my eardrums in a staccato beat.

Then a single deep word to my heart reverberates inside like an orchestra's timpani building to a resounding crescendo: *Come.*

Hear it again; feel it in your chest.

My friend told me of the oasis. It must be near. I feel the urgency within me now, cheering me on. I walk faster, confident now that I'm on the path God wants me to follow, not some mad chase. Where is He leading me? Where will I end up? It matters little—only that I'm going where He wants me.

I grin a little, amazed at my confidence that just a moment ago had so completely disappeared...like the stream emerging in the desert.

It has been a long time since I've felt this way—"too long, Lord," I whisper—so long since I've been so clear on where I'm going. This is why I'm here. To know Him again. To feel His presence. To remember.

"Come," He beckons again. "Come."

I grin, wondering at the wisdom of so recklessly seeking a meeting with the living God. But what could be wiser? I can't shrink back now.

He has called.

I will answer.

I turn one way, then another, then again, wondering if I'm going in circles in this crazy, mazelike cavern. The channel narrows to a point that I have to turn sideways to fit through, and a frightening vision of a flash flood fills my head. Floods can send a twelve-foot wall of water coursing through canyons like this—

"Come," He calls. "Come, My precious child."

Again and again the path widens, then narrows. With each turn I hear Him beckoning, making my heart beat faster each time, until all at once, everything is silent. I turn in a slow circle, waiting, longing to hear His voice again.

"Lord?" I whisper.

Hear yourself whispering to Him. Then again, a little louder.

I hurry forward, wondering if I've made a mistake, somehow missed a critical turn...

"L-Lord?" I shy backward when the sound of my voice echoes and echoes...

I peek farther around the corner, and my breath catches

in my throat. It's what my friend called the cathedral. The oasis. My passageway opens into a great hall, the vaulted, straight walls uncommon in this gulch of curves and arcs. On the other side is a deep pool of water, and at its edges, cottonwood and alder and scrub oaks are in full leaf. But that's on the other side. Directly before me is a boxed canyon with rock sides that converge overhead, almost shutting out the sky to create a cavernlike room.

It's royal. Awe inspiring.

Nearby a creek trickles down the rock to meet the red-stained water at my feet, its sound like the Vespers hymn of a far-off monastery. Desert varnish—a lustrous patina of iron and manganese oxides—streaks and stains the walls in a living tapestry worthy of the King. The markings come down in broad bands like pennons on a castle wall.

Afternoon sunshine floods the cave and canyon walls, suffusing them with unearthly red-golden light like I've never before witnessed. It makes the rock glow like a living flame.

To the right, where the fresh water of the creek from above meets the silty creek at my feet, lush green vines spring to life and spread out, one on top of another in a mad testimony of life where life shouldn't be.

I've arrived. I fall to my knees in the damp sand.

He is here. I can feel His approach. Sense it.

What does it feel like?

I turn away briefly to quench my thirst, then turn again to the cathedral to witness my King coming closer. The sun continues along its path, and the light floods the titanic chambers in a glowing, delicate pink. As it moves, it sends a shaft of ethereal light to the center of the chamber, reminding me of a shard of sunlight piercing a dense cloud hovering over the plains.

"Come," I hear again.

I stumble forward, my heart beating faster and faster in fear and awe at His presence. I remind myself to breathe.

Deep breathe in…and out.

Cautiously, I approach the light. This is why I've come, why I had to come. The entire reason I'm meant to be here.

I sink to my knees again in the damp, heavy sand and raise my hands to the heavenly One who so clearly watches over me. I close my eyes in the blinding light and feel its warmth wash over me.

Feel the heat flowing over you, through you, surrounding you.

"Thank You," I whisper.

Silently thank Him.

What does He say to you? Can you hear His words of love?

Let God's words nourish your soul, fill your heart.
Does it make you smile? Have you ever felt anything like this?
Do you feel your scalp tingling at His nearness?

All at once, the sins of my heart cloud my happiness, dim my joy.

Silently confess your sins to Him. Everything.

As I confess, I become aware of a gentle breeze edging down the canyon. It isn't the frightening roar of the sandstorm, but the quieter, soothing sound and feel of an ocean wind. It's as if He's responding to the words of my heart.

What is He saying to you in response?

The wind increases, but this time no sand pelts my face. My hair swirls around my head madly as if I'm in the middle of a vacuum. It sweeps over me, above me, away from me, and with it go the sins, the burdens of my confession.

Hear God's message of grace and cleansing through Christ.
You've been set free.

From the sins of your youth. From the sins of the past year.
From the sins of yesterday. From the sins of this day.

Feel the wind wash over your face
and down your arms and away, away, away...

Deep breathe in...and out.

In...and out.

I remember why I've come. "Thank You for drawing near, Lord. Thank You for reminding me of who You are. I forget so quickly. I forget that You're nearby, always ready to walk alongside me. Help me to remember."

Memorize this moment, this feeling of sitting
in His quiet, covering, reassuring embrace. Of being held
from head to toe. Of being known and loved inside out.

"Help me not to hide from You, Father. Help me to remember and ask You closer each day. Amen."

I open my eyes and realize the shaft of light is fading. I feel the last vestiges of warmth on my face like a lover's departing caress to my cheek.

"Thank You, Father, for bringing me here. Thank You for showing me the way."

The vanishing light betrays the shallow steps, in shadow now, along the southern cliff face, the remnants of shepherds who have run their sheep through this uncommon canyon. The way will be somewhat precarious, but I know I can make it.

The canyon is chilling now in the fast-falling desert dusk. Handhold by handhold, toehold by toehold, I climb out of the desert cathedral. I emerge on a ridge and gasp as I crest the top and find my footing on the rocks. The sky is the color of the sandstone canyon I've just left behind—a swirling soup of tomato and pepper hues.

God isn't only in the canyon below; He is here with me now. Always and forever.

I smile again, feeling refreshed and surer of my next steps than ever before. "Goodnight, Father," I whisper. "I hope You're coming with me." Then I turn toward home.

Amen. ✍

Chapter Six

AT THE BEACH HOUSE

WHEN YOU YEARN FOR HIS COMPANY

With thanks to Robert Boyd Munger
for his insightful book, *My Heart, Christ's Home,*
and the inspiration it has lent me.

God is a faithful friend.

PSALM 146; I CORINTHIANS 1:9

Be still before the Lord: After getting comfortable, practice deep, slow breathing for a minute or two. Then turn on an inspirational song of faith with words or music that unfailingly move you. Concentrate on each note as it emerges from your stereo, as if it were created just for you.

Reflect: This end-of-the-day exercise is called "review of the day." Begin with the morning and move forward through your day—or begin at the present time and move backward—hour by hour. Consider each conversation, each expression or emotion, and what God might have been saying to you in the moment through other people and through your own senses and thoughts.

This is at least a five-minute exercise. Go slowly. Don't rush it. Hour by hour.

Enter into prayer: As you read through the following beach scene, pause periodically to focus on your senses and bring this scene to life. Use these pauses to stop and consider sight, smell, sound, and touch. Read each sentence slowly, pausing often to dwell upon the meaning for you.

Take a deep, slow breath. In and out, in and out.

Lord God, as I begin to pray, help me to recognize You in my life, in the everyday as well as in the unique. Help me to be open to learning more about You every moment. Forgive me my unbelief, Lord. Come to me, now. Show me who You are. And keep evil far from me. In Jesus' name. Amen.

THE BEACH HOUSE has been in my family for decades. It could be any house, really, but it was built by my great-grandfather, maintained by my grandparents, and remodeled by my parents. Now it belongs to me alone. It's here, by the ocean, that I come to feel my connection to the people who have loved me all my life on earth and to the God who will love me beyond it.

I trudge along the tide-hewn hills of sand, intent on finding just the right place to perch. Finding it, I sit down with my feet before me, knees tucked under my arms, just at the water's edge. I watch the sun sink into the ocean. The gentle waves crest and roll forward in a mad, hopeful dash toward land. Then they slow, pull up, and recede.

I dig my toes into the wet grains of sand, feeling them mold to every curve of my feet—the damp, wet chill of last night's high tide seeping into my skin.

*Imagine yourself there, smelling the salt,
feeling the approach of night's cooling temperatures.*

There's no one else on the beach, and I take a deep breath, the smells of salt and fish and water on the wind all rushing through my nose.

It's the end of the season, and the summer people are long gone. The beach belongs only to me and a few other year-rounders.

The sunset's hues soon fade from mandarin orange and nectarine red to a more subdued peach and pastel yellow. The water still dances with the quiet colors, but I shiver and head back to the house. Without the sun, it's chilly. Bone-chilling, damp cold. Time for something hot to drink, some quiet music, and some time on the enclosed porch of the house.

Feel a shiver run down your spine, the urgency for warmth and shelter.

I quickly climb the rickety wooden steps silvered by wind, sun, and salt. They double back repeatedly up the steep hillside that hovers over the sand. I pull open the sand-roughened wood door and close it behind me with some relief.

The sounds of the waves are still audible, but a crackling, welcoming fire I've left burning in the fireplace soon eases away the chill from my clothing and cheeks and hands.

Padding into the kitchen in stocking feet, I set the teapot on the gas stove and watch as a blue flame ignites and surrounds the kettle's bottom.

The house is quiet, except for the fire in the living room and the flickering stove before me. I fight off a wave of utter loneliness, the kind of unwelcome solitude you feel when you're awake at 3 A.M. and nobody else is.

"You've called me here, Lord, to this place," I whisper. "What do You want to tell me?"

Silently ask Him now what He wants to say to you.

I've been called away from my chaotic life, from days filled with appointments and schedules and phone meetings. Of demands and chores and desires. To this. This quiet, simple, old house. Along the edges of the deep. My eyes follow down the hallway to the glass wall that fronts the living room. The ocean, from this vantage point, looks slightly convex; I can see the curvature of the earth's surface. I'm a tiny speck on this great, big planet. What am I to the Creator?

"Why do You want me to know You, Jesus? Why do You yearn for my company as much as I yearn for Yours? I'm nothing, so insignificant! In this huge, wide world, I'm infinitesimal."

The teapot whistles, and I jump, startled.

I shake my head, but as I pour the hot water over the fragrant tea leaves, watching the color dance and seep into the clear, I realize that's what I want most—such a deep companionship with God that His being infuses my own.

Fighting off a feeling of foolishness, I kneel there in my kitchen and bow my head. "Make me like a mug of water," I pray, "with You, Jesus, as the tea. Enter my heart, infuse me with the taste, the smell of You. Make me Your own, Lord. Make me Your own."

Silently repeat that prayer of request.

A warm presence covers me, as physically tangible as the steaming liquid that trickles down my throat.

Take a moment to sense His presence close to you. Covering you. Surrounding you. Soaking into you. Keep tightly in your mind the image of the tea infusing the water with its color and taste and smell.

I smile. "Thank You, Father, for drawing near. Stay with me. Show me what You want me to learn and remember." What He can teach me is ancient knowledge, something I've always known at some level—but I've forgotten. I hunger for it. *Need* to know it again.

I rise from my knees, taking the mug from the counter and walking to the living room, still feeling my Savior as He walks beside me. My loneliness has mixed with the intense spiritual wave that has covered me and dissipated. He is present. All-encompassing. Everything else is washed away. There's utter peace within, without.

I settle into a cozy, cushy couch and look out to sea. My earlier question of why He would want to know me—one of billions on this big blue planet—surfaces again.

> *Take a moment to see Him settle in right beside you and offer you a brotherly hand. What does His hand feel like in yours? What do His eyes say to you?*

For the first time, no matter how many times I've heard it before, it strikes me that He would die for me. For me alone. That if I were the only one on this great, big world, He would do it again. The cross. The horror of that day. *For me.*

The thought brings quick tears to my eyes. I sink from the couch to the floor, at His knees. "No, Lord. No. I'm unworthy."

He speaks for the first time. "I have made you worthy. Through Me, you are redeemed."

"Please Father, I'm not worth it. I have sinned. I will sin again—I know myself that much."

> *Feel Him lift your chin, look into your eyes. Dare to look back.*

"Hear these words," He quietly demands.

> *Hear Him say your name.*

"You've asked Me in. I've made you Mine. You belong to Me. There's nothing that can dissuade Me or take Me from your side. Nothing."

He is promising the impossible. People in my life have disappointed me, betrayed me. But this person—God—will not. I know it as truth as surely as I know my hand is connected to my wrist. It's undefeatable, undebatable, undisguised, naked truth. Honesty in its purest form. He'll never stray from my side. He knows me. He knows where I fall short. And He still loves me without restraint. He's my constant companion. Forevermore.

> *Confess to Him where you fall short.*
> *Though He knows them already, lay your sins at His feet.*

When I'm done, He rises and offers me a hand, assisting me to my feet. He takes His hands and cradles either side of my face, looking deep into my eyes. At first I imagine I must struggle to keep my focus and not look away—but indeed, I couldn't if I tried. Looking into His eyes is like seeing into the depths of the ocean. It's mesmerizing.

"You're forgiven," He promises. And the forgiveness washes through me like the sound of an ocean wave, pulling the darkness of my heart back out to the depths.

He gestures toward the sunroom. I enter the glass-covered room overlooking the precipice of the ocean's cliff. Before us is the dim, fading light of the setting sun, now in colors of palest coffee and cream above a taupe sea. High above, the stars are beginning to emerge. Below, the waves crash in vivid white slosh, fading and cresting, fading and cresting.

But it's out to the distant salt waters that He points.

> *Feel His presence near you, Him holding your hand.*
> *Look out to sea with the new eyes that He gives you.*
> *Do you feel safe but on the edge of an adventure?*

"It's there that I want you to go," He tells me, still pointing. I spot the dim outline of a sailing vessel, barely discernible in the distance, her triangular canvas filled full in a far-off breeze.

"Where, Father?"

"There," He insists. And with Him at my side, I see where He's directing.

Where is He sending you? To do what? Take a moment to consider it.

"I cannot, Lord," I say. "Send someone else. It isn't in me."

No, not in me—*but in Him.* Scripture comes to mind: "For in him you have been enriched in every way—in all your speaking and in all your knowledge—because our testimony about Christ was confirmed in you.... God, who has called you into fellowship with his Son Jesus Christ our Lord, is faithful."

I lean hard on His arm, but He supports me as if I weigh nothing at all. "I will obey," I whisper. "Make me like that sailing ship, with You the breeze, and I will follow Your direction,

Lord." With Him, all things are truly possible. He will make the way. He'll see me through.

Whisper your promise to Him.

I rub my eyes, weary from head to toe. The light has dimmed to twilight, the stars now more numerous in a velvet sky. He leads me to the bedroom, and sleepily, I slip into the cool, smooth sheets and lie back. He covers me then with the old, down-filled quilt that smells just right. Like home. I feel completely safe but fighting curious shame, with Him right here in my bedroom—*of all places.*

I dare to look up at Him again; the light of the hallway surrounds Him in a warm halo, and He smiles a gentle smile. For the first time, it hits me that He already knows all about me and still loves me. I've confessed my sins, and He has forgiven me. For everything.

Take His offered grace and love—immerse yourself in it.
Ask Him to help you keep taking it in, in every situation.
Ask Him for the strength to do all He asks of you, and promise
Him you'll do it, knowing He'll help you along the way.

He pauses at the base of my bed, then gently touches the lump that my toes make. "My Word is a lamp to your feet. Remember."

Promise Him that you'll seek His Word.

He moves near my knees and hips, gesturing toward them. I can almost feel the weight they've been bearing in a pulsing ache, as if I've hiked many miles this day, instead of only a short stroll on the beach.

It's the weariness of a decade's trials.

"I give strength to the weary," He says knowingly.

Promise that you'll lean on Him instead of yourself.
Ask Him to help you do this.

He comes ever closer and places a light hand on my chest, above my heart. "If I live here, you'll never miss Me again. And if you listen to your heart, you will hear Me." After a long moment, He touches my head, as if in blessing.

"Keep your thoughts on whatever is true, whatever is noble, whatever is right, whatever is pure, whatever is lovely, whatever is admirable—if anything is excellent or praise-worthy—think about such things. Whatever you have learned or received or heard from me, or seen in me—put it into practice. And the God of peace will be with you."

Staring up into His eyes, I say, "Lord God, help me to remember Your presence in the intimacy of my bedroom. Help me to remember all of what You've said."

"I will," He promises, laying a salutary hand on my

shoulder. He leans down and whispers in my ear. "Remember I am with you, always. Know Me, and you will remember My ways.

"Close your eyes now, child, and sleep."

"I will, Father. I will."

I take a deep, long breath, then smile as I hear Him quietly leave the room.

Take a deep breath in...and out.

I peek once more, willing weary eyelids open, hoping to catch a last glimpse of Him. My room is dark and cool, but in the hallway, through a doorway opened a few inches, is a bright, warm light. I focus on it for a long moment, taking deep breaths.

Breathe in...breathe out, focusing on the light.

"I will," I say, repeating my promise. "I will remember You and all Your ways."

With that, I fall into a deep, peaceful sleep.

Father God, thank You for making a home of my heart. Thank you for teaching me Your ways when I open the door and ask You to come in.

Help me to be a person of memory—memorizing Your ways, Your Word, and keeping my promises to You. Help me to remember what it's like to live in Your presence each and every day. In Jesus' name I pray. Amen. ✄

Chapter Seven

THE PARDONING

WHEN YOU NEED TO LEAVE JUSTICE IN GOD'S HANDS

God is just.

PSALM 11; JAMES 4:11-12

Be still before the Lord: Take a minute to sit and clear your mind, stretching, releasing the stress from neck and shoulders and back. Remember to practice full breathing.

Once you've quieted yourself before God, kneel before Him or consider the idea of stretching out on the ground, face-down, spread-eagled—in recognition of making yourself totally vulnerable to Him. Do this in a secure and private place (such as your locked bedroom), without fear of discovery; the only One you want to discover you is God.

Deep breathe in...and out. Close your eyes and concentrate on being before the throne of God. He is everywhere. He is before you now.

Say, "Lord Jesus Christ, Son of God, have mercy upon me, a sinner." Repeat this over and over as you concentrate on how the position of kneeling or being prostrate makes you feel, and what these words mean in this context. Repeat "Lord Jesus Christ, Son of God, have mercy upon me, a sinner" for as long as you feel is necessary.

Rise to your knees. Then stretch out again, repeating the ancient prayer.

Feel His mercy begin to fill you, cover you.

Rise.

Deep breathe in...and out.

Read and reflect: Consider this quote from contemplative master Thomas Merton: "We will never be anything else but beginners all of our life." If a master of prayer and spirituality said that, what does that mean for the rest of us?

Enter into prayer: *Maker of heaven, help me banish my feelings of injustice, knowing that You can take care of everything. Help me, through this prayer, to see things as You see them and to rest in your timing. Block the Father of Lies, and fill me with Your truth. Amen.*

EVERY YEAR I return to the hot springs. I gather up my camping supplies—a tiny pup tent I've had for twenty years, a sleeping bag that smells like the basement, a small kerosene stove, flashlight, food, and water bottles. Then I drive the three hours out a lonely highway that stretches for miles in one straight ribbon, then turns into tight, fifteen-mile-per-hour curves.

Eventually I'm climbing into the trees, later into old-growth forest. And I continue to climb in my car...up, up, up the mountain...making the engine churn as hard as my mind has been churning.

I always know when it's time for my hot springs trip. There's either a big decision to make, a life getting too crazy to handle without my turning into a raging maniac, or God's working on my mind and heart.

What's going on in your life right now? Is God working on your mind? Your heart? Trying to get you to come to terms with something? Something that deals with forgiveness?

This year I think it's God who's sending me on my way. Two days ago I happened to read this in *The Message:* "Don't grieve God. Don't break his heart. His Holy Spirit, moving and breathing in you, is the most intimate part of your life, making you fit for himself. Don't take such a gift for granted.

"Make a clean break with all cutting [and] backbiting.... Be gentle with one another, sensitive. Forgive one another as quickly and thoroughly as God in Christ forgave you."

It's from Ephesians 4. I do a morning devotional every day, but lately I haven't felt like doing anything that's moving in God's direction. I'm tired. Worn out. And that snippet really made me angry. It's assuming that everything that's been done to me can be forgiven. It places the responsibility back in *my* lap. And it invokes Christ's name to bring the point home. Doesn't He know? Doesn't He know exactly how I've been wronged? Surely He doesn't expect me to forgive this!

*Consider something someone did to you
in the past that has been difficult to forgive.*

I roll my head as I drive, trying to relieve some of the tension. I don't know what I'm doing here, why I'm on this highway at all. I'm too worked up to really work through anything. But I can't explain it. I just had to come.

"Okay, Lord," I mutter, looking out the top of my windshield where a bright robin's-egg blue sky meets the green treetops. I can give Him twenty-four hours. I'm not hopeful, but He's worked that fast before. Maybe He can do something with me this time too.

*See yourself in that car, driving, driving, letting the road
begin to ease some of your tension. See yourself giving God
a little leeway, the slightest opportunity, to work in you.*

A half-hour later I arrive at the campground. As expected, it's nearly deserted. This time of year, few people come to this most favored of sites. There's one other tent pitched already, and a second one is going up. I doubt anybody else will arrive. Darkness is just around the corner.

I choose a triangulated point away from the other two campers, to give us all maximum privacy, and I say a quick prayer of hope that they don't know the way to my hot springs. There are many springs about, drawing in campers from all around the state, but few know of my sanctuary.

The late afternoon is spent in making camp, then a simple dinner. I stare at my Bible in the fading light, hoping to find some revelation on why I've been sent here, what He wants me to figure out. But I see the words on the page as stark and distant, irrelevant.

Darkness falls fast this time of year, and soon I'm staring at the pages by the light of my lamp, an evening breeze rustling their edges. The words blur and swim in front of me; my mind is on a hundred things other than the task before me.

> *Take a moment to concentrate on why God has brought*
> *you here. Who He wants you to forgive. Contemplate what*
> *it would mean to forgive that person, and eradicate,*
> *one by one, all the details that cascade through your mind.*

It's impossible. It's too big. When I was hurt, I was cut to the core, sliced open, eviscerated.

> *What was done to you? Did you feel humiliated?*
> *Betrayed? Cut down? Bludgeoned?*
> *Mowed over, totally? Name all that you felt in the hurt.*

The wind has a wintry chill to it, and I soon turn into my pup tent and zip up the door, noting that my neighbors are either already asleep or off to the hot springs. I've paid them little attention and haven't even bothered to go over and introduce myself. I'm not interested in superficial camaraderie around a campfire this night. Perhaps they feel the same.

The wind begins howling through the trees. As much as my body is tired, longing for sleep, my mind is awake. I wonder if a branch will break off in the wind and crash onto my tent. I wonder if the wind will bring rain, even though none was forecast. Freak storms come in a place like this. I shift, over and over I shift, having picked the rockiest campsite I've ever tried to sleep on. First a bulge bothers me at my lower back, then another below my right shoulder blade, and so on and so on.

In the dark and with the wind howling, see yourself in that tent, aching to sleep but unable to rest. Switching positions. Over and over.

All night I seem to barely get to sleep, then I awaken. My eyelids lift again and again as a gust rages through the forest, engulfs me, then passes. I fear the stakes will be pulled up, my tent ripped and swimming around me like a suffocating cocoon. Every time I think it's going to ebb, the storm flows.

Ripping, ripping, ripping. I feel attacked. Naked in the storm.

"What?" I whisper.

Hear yourself whisper it now, the sound lost in the wind.

"What do You want from me?" I say aloud.

Hear yourself say it aloud.

"Father, tell me!" I shout. Even the sound of my shout is like a drop of water in the midst of a lake.

Hear your voice, lost in the storm, calling out to your heavenly Father.

"Tell me...just tell me. Tell me, tell me, tell me. I want to sleep. I want to rest. Show me. In Jesus' name."

There's no answer, but gradually I notice that the windstorm is abating. Yet the more I have the opportunity to sleep, the more awake I seem to be. Sighing heavily, I rise and pull on my swimsuit, then a sweatshirt, and finally my sneakers. I pick up my flashlight, glance at my watch, and sigh. Four-thirty. No sane person wakes at four-thirty for the day.

So much for a night of much-sought-after peace. My only hope of reprieve is the hot spring. My only hope is to enter the warm waters and feel the peace seep into my soul.

See yourself leaving the tent, the lonely golden beam from the flashlight before you.

The other tents are dark, their inhabitants perhaps asleep, now that the wind has died. I should've done as they had, gone to the hot springs before the storm blew through. I would've been so relaxed, I could have slept through anything.

What's done is done, I tell myself, and move along the well-worn path. About a half-mile farther, I see the marker that my father's father showed him and that he once pointed out to me. In the pale luminosity of my flashlight, I see the shape of a large granite rock. It's always reminded me of an angel's wing. That's what Dad called it too.

I veer off, careful to not disturb the plants or rocks beneath my feet. We want it to remain a family secret, this place. Let the others have the numerous, well-marked springs. This place is ours. I duck under a tree branch, then two others. I maneuver around several towering boulders, including the Angel Wing rock, now indistinguishable against the other rockfaces. Up ahead is the gash, a V in the rocks that always reminds me of a heavenly split. I wouldn't be surprised if God's hand were in this place. Every time I enter, I find myself changed.

I pause at the V and take a deep, slow breath. Am I ready to really face what I must?

Breathe deeply, slowly...
Are you ready to face the truth of your situation?

I plunge ahead without waiting any longer. To question my path is to face defeat. I must move forward. The only other way is backward.

Ten steps farther and I'm there. In this tiny arena, rounded rocks and boulders all about me, is a hot spring. Faint sulfur smells fill the air, but it isn't as bad as in other places I've been. I pull off my sweatshirt and my sneakers and set them on a rock beside me. The declining moon is almost down for the night, making way for the sun, but from this angle it illuminates the entire steaming pool.

A faint breeze moves the trees, setting the light on the water to a shimmering, skipping silver across the top. But it's muted on and off because of the steam that rolls off the top.

Suddenly, I feel the ache in my bones from my toes to my scalp. Worse than that, I feel the heavy weight of my heart, the burden. I can't wait to get into the water. To feel it cover me. To find God's answers. To find His intimate Spirit, moving and breathing in me, but currently stifled.

> *See yourself touch the hot water with your toes,*
> *at first wincing at the heat, then dipping again. Feel it*
> *as a welcome, inviting warmth now, as it covers your body.*

The bottom is gritty but fairly smooth. The waters have worn away a sculpted pool for me, with a long crevasse down the center that I imagine extends deep, deep down through the earth's crust. It is God's earth that heats my pool. His water. His creation. And I am His creation.

"I'm sorry," I whisper, rubbing hot, wet hands across my weary eyes. I watch the moonlight continue to shimmer on the water. But it's paling. To the east, the sunrise encroaches on night's territory.

"I know I've been stubborn," I say. The sound of my voice is at once amplified over the water as well as slightly muffled by the heavy water particles of steam. I shift in the pool to the other side so I can watch the rising sun. At this point, it's a mere golden glow on the horizon, pushing back the dark.

"I don't think You understand. It hurt. It hurt so much."

Pour out to Him the depths of your pain, the grief you've suffered because of what this other person has done to you.

"They haven't paused. They haven't looked back. It isn't fair."

Tell Him of your complaint.

Deep breathe in...and out.

Hear now His words to you about forgiveness.

How He forgave you.

How in forgiving this other person, you'll find freedom. See how your hold on injustice has grieved God, broken His heart, blocked His Spirit.

Deep breathe in...and out.

Suddenly it's not about my forgiving this other person. It's about God forgiving me.

I ponder on that a moment, truly surprised by the thought. It's not about forgiving them, it's more about God forgiving me. Will I ever get this faith thing figured out? What kind of example am I, holding on to this darkness with a stubborn iron fist?

"I'm sorry," I whisper. "I'm sorry."

A single tear slips down my cheek. In apologizing to God, I've found room in my heart to forgive other sinners. They're no different than I. And it's for God to set them straight, not my place to do so. I don't have to see it through. I don't have to see justice done.

God has us all in His hands. Like this big bowl that now holds me and suspends me in hot water, God holds all of us.

With my hands in front of me, I clench them as tightly I can, for as long as I can.

Feel your fists clench. Imagine holding inside them frustration, your hurt, your pain, your grief.

I look to the rising sun, her glory shining in high, hot pink clouds and fading darkness. Directly above me, the brightest stars are still visible. I look again to the sun, her top just peeking over the rocks. Then I look down to my hands. And slowly, ever so slowly, I open them.

See your fingers roll outward, the empty space of your palms.

Water covers them, warms them, heals them.

And in the emptiness, I find a hint of peace.

I let myself slip beneath the waters, feeling the heat cover my scalp and ease away the stress and tenseness. Then I rise and take in the periwinkle sky and clouds that are now cotton-candy pink. In my mind's eye I see myself forgiving the people who have wronged me. Forgiving as Jesus would—with a peaceful hand upon the shoulder, a gentle word.

For the first time it's within my reach. A possibility.

For the first time in a long time, I feel I can take a full breath.

Deep breathe in...and out.

I breathe again, feeling the heat work into my muscles and bones and joints to relax them, heal them.

Breathe in...and out.

The water suddenly seems too hot. It's time to go home. It's time to move on. I rise and make my way out of the pool and stand at its edge, gazing toward the sun.

Free. Forgiven. And ready to forgive.

Breathe in...and out.

Amen. ✍

Chapter Eight

THE CONQUEROR

WHEN THE BATTLE IS TOO MUCH FOR YOU

God is all-powerful.

REVELATION 19:6

Be still before the Lord: Take deep breaths, in...and out. Let your mind cascade through your history as you do this, thinking about each year of your life as best as you can remember them. (This is not a test; it's an exercise.) Consider principal people in your life, your jobs, your faith life. Are there any people you fell away from? Any disagreements that you never resolved?

Sit down and write three notes or letters to people with whom you don't have something resolved. Pray about it. Ask the Father to guide you in whether you should actually send the notes to those long-lost friends, family members, or an old boyfriend or girlfriend. If you've lost track of these people, or if you decide it would be more disruptive than constructive to contact them, ask the Lord to give them the peace and knowledge that *you* have forgiven them and moved on yourself.

Burn these letters in your fireplace, and as you watch them shrivel and blacken, release those sorrowful memories into God's care. Ask Him to forgive you for your role in those problems. Rest in the knowledge that you're forgiven and freed!

Read and reflect:

> Rest on this earth is false rest. Beware of
> those who urge you to find happiness here;
> you won't find it. Guard against the false
> physicians who promise that joy is only a
> diet away, a marriage away, a job away.... Try
> this. Imagine a perfect world. Whatever that
> means for you, imagine it. Does that mean
> peace? Then envision absolute tranquility.
> Does a perfect world imply joy? Then create
> your highest happiness. Will a perfect world
> have love? If so, ponder a place where love
> has no bounds. Whatever heaven means to
> you, imagine it. Get it firmly fixed in your
> mind.... And then smile as the Father re-
> minds you, *No one has ever imagined what God
> has prepared for those who love him....* When it
> comes to describing heaven, we are all happy
> failures. (Max Lucado, *When God Whispers
> Your Name*)

Spend five minutes doing as Max Lucado suggests in the
passage above. Is there something troubling you right now,
something you're struggling with, that makes you long for
heaven? We make our way as best we can on earth, but

heaven will bring us restored health, restored relationships, perfect peace.

Enter into prayer: Take a deep, slow breath. In and out, in and out.

Father in heaven, help me rest in the knowledge that You're ever present, always with me. In the midst of the storms of life, help me lean on You and seek Your direction. You are the Alpha and Omega. When my struggles threaten to get the best of me, to overwhelm me, help me focus on You.

And in the midst of this prayer, as I think on my struggle and on You, keep the Evil One at bay. Amen.

I'VE ALWAYS LOVED the mountains in wintertime. The hush of a full blanket of snow, pines laden with marshmallow, miles of land with not a single visible track. Sheer heaven.

I pull my car off the highway and switch to four-wheel drive. The snow is deeper on this turnoff, the trees lending shade throughout the season, keeping it from melting. It's heavy and clings to my tires, but I move on through, slipping and sliding a bit, but making headway nonetheless.

In the summer, I hike this trail, appreciating the heat of the sun, the fresh smell of fertile land, wildlife at every turn. But in the winter—in the winter this land has the clean purity of a silver bell, the fresh draw of a mountain spring. It's irresistible.

I pull to a stop, shift into park, and grab my backpack. No one else in sight. Indeed, it looks like no one has been here in a month. Just the way I like it.

I open my car door and check the snow. It's about a foot deep, and I'm glad for my waterproof boots. From the back of my vehicle I pull out my snowshoes and strap them on. They're lightweight, and I'm immediately on top of the deep drifts. Securing my backpack straps for good weight distribution, I set off.

See yourself there. Feel the weight of your backpack, the odd pacing and sounds of your snowshoes. The crunch of the snow.

I like to pretend I'm a French trapper or a pioneer when I'm out here. It's just me, my supplies, nature, and God. There's something refining in experiencing such a moment.

Consider how it would feel to be all alone in the wild. Or remember a time when you were. Recall the feelings you experienced. Self-reliance? Exhilaration? Peace? Pride? What? Deep breathe in...and out.

I get into my pace, intending to hike five miles in. The weather report is good. A slight chance of snow, but nothing I can't manage. I'm prepared. Right now the sky is clear and blue and beautiful. The sun glints off the pristine white snow in a dazzling display of nature's purity. Blue shadows hide behind rocks. There's a slight breeze, just enough to nudge mounds of snow off limbs and send them cascading down in a flurry of white. The snow thumps as it hits the drifts below. It's a dull, lonely sound.

My breath comes in a quick panting rhythm now that sounds good to me, reminding me I'm alive. Life, really living, has seemed illusory to me lately. If I didn't have this current battle on my hands, I'd be more conscious of it more often.

What are you battling now? Illness? Something at work? Something with your family? Name it now in your heart.

Instead, I'm caught in the cycle of decay. Putting on Band-Aids where I need a full cast. Yet no one seems to notice. No one seems to care. Not even my closest friends or my family can fully empathize with me. What it's like to be me. What's it's like to deal with this.

My snowshoes break through the crisp upper layer of snow, each step a clean crunch through the crust. The loneliness of my struggle hits me, like a slow tear down my cheek in the night. I call out to God. "Lord, why are You so far from me?"

Feel the loneliness, the isolation as you see yourself showshoe up a hill...through a valley...mile after mile...

My breathing is labored, but I'm determined to reach the crest of the next hill, a saddle that I know will reward me with an amazing view. Perhaps there I will meet my Father, the One who can show me my way through.

I reach the crest, breaking through the trees and looking across acres of forest before me. But the mountains beyond are shrouded in gray clouds, evidence of a storm quickly approaching. I sigh in frustration. The view is one of my favorite parts of the hike, one of the main reasons I come here. Today, even the weather is working against me.

> *Feel the disappointment of this moment on the ridge.*
> *Of hopes now dashed after a series of disappointments.*

As I stand, catching my breath, I wonder why God can't give me what I hoped for. After all I've been through lately, can't He come through here?

> *Express your frustration with the*
> *Lord over your own situation now.*

The snow begins falling, and I close my eyes to feel the gentle sting of each flake. It's blowing in fast, this storm. A few flurries, they said. Not a full-blown winter storm. *Perfect,* I think sarcastically.

I look over my shoulder. Four and a half miles from the car. Then I look forward. I'm a half-mile away from my destination, a picturesque meadow surrounded by glacier-carved peaks, one of those places where I always feel God come close.

My eyes travel back to the clouds, but I can't see very

well, since the snow is coming down hard now. I pull up my hood and zip up my jacket to better cover my neck and chin. As much as I want to get to my meadow, I need to go back to the car. Even if I got to the meadow, I wouldn't be able to see a thing. It's the wise choice to turn back. The safe choice. The smart choice.

I sigh.

> *Feel yourself sigh, giving up on your goal,*
> *just the latest of several setbacks.*

I turn around and head back down the hill. The snow is blowing all around me, the wind picking up, bringing down the snow from the trees as well as the sky. *It isn't fair,* I think. I came here to find some comfort from God, some way out of my struggle, and instead it feels like He's driving me away.

Bitter tears blur my vision as much as the snow. Life has been tough enough lately...

I plow forward, hurrying now, realizing I could get caught out here. It could be deadly. I wouldn't be the first well-prepared hiker to get stuck in a sudden mountain storm. Rescuers couldn't get to me in this weather.

Adrenaline surges through my limbs, urging me on.

My tracks are easily visible for a while, but soon I can't make them out any longer. Blowing snow has filled them in. I look around, trying to get my bearings, make out land-marks, but to no avail.

The clouds are low. The wind ferocious. The snow blinding.

For the first time this day, I know fear.

I think I see a tree I remember, one that was split long ago by lightning, and I head in that direction. If only I had my compass! When I reach the old ponderosa pine, however, I realize it's not the tree I remembered.

Again a shiver of fright rolls down my spine.

> *See yourself there, in the midst of a blinding storm, looking about in a slow circle, suddenly feeling overwhelmed and scared.*

I decide this will not get the best of me. I've walked in these mountains countless times before. Certainly I can make my way out again! I'll figure it out. I set off again, walking a hundred paces, squinting my eyes to get a better look at the terrain.

But I still don't recognize anything.

It has to be this way... I walk and walk. My watch shows that the hours are disappearing, but I don't feel as if I'm anywhere close to where I think I should be. Not that I can see a thing. The snow is blinding and it doesn't appear to be letting up.

I must seek shelter. In my pack I have an emergency food bar, a foil blanket, water. If I can get out of the elements, I can await rescue or hike out myself tomorrow. If I can just do this...

Lord, show me the way, I pray silently. *Show me where to find shelter.*

> *Hear yourself praying that prayer.*

I hike over a hill and find a large rock outcropping. I crouch under it and discover that most of the wind and snow is blocked here. Nearby is a young tree with lush but slender limbs. Going to it, I cut off five of the limbs with my knife and drag them to the outcropping. Positioning these branches on either side of the rock overhang, I create a small room. This is my best bet for survival.

Please Lord, let me survive this night, I pray.

> *Hear yourself praying this prayer too. Tell your Father about how this is too much; on top of everything else, it's simply too much. Tell Him of your need, your desire for Him to rescue you. To be the conqueror in this latest battle. Deep breathe in...and out.*

I reinforce the walls, then cover the doorway with the last of the branches. I roll up in my foil emergency blanket, feeling the winter chill of the rocks entering my bones. How long will it take to warm up? Will I ever warm up?

As I rest my cheek against the grainy texture of my backpack, I wonder if I will die here. Succumb to the elements. Dimly, I resign myself to it: If I die, at least my battle will be over. I'll be with Jesus.

The wind howls past my cave, working on those branches I placed above me, threatening to tear them away. I realize I'm not thinking clearly. Hypothermia must be setting in.

"Father God," I whisper, my teeth chattering. "I'm losing it. I'm losing the battle. If You want me to survive, I need You to intervene. I can't win this alone. I need You, Jesus. Save me, save me, save me."

Silently echo this prayer. Deep breathe in...and out.

Deep inside, I feel the tiniest bit of warmth in my belly, and it spreads outward. My eyelids are leaden, begging me to sleep. Part of the hypothermia, I guess. Sleep could very well mean death. But it's so tempting, everything I want right now, to close my eyes and sleep... I have to stay awake, stay awake, stay awake...

Feel your heavy eyelids, your deep, slow breathing, the desire to give in to sleep.

I'm getting warmer. The heat is spreading through my extremities. Either that or my mind is lying, seducing me into a frozen death. I've heard the stories. Feeling warm as they die...but I'm just so tired, exhausted. I can't do it anymore. Any of it. "Father, I need You. I need You. I need You."

Repeat the prayer of petition silently. Whatever your battle, ask God to enter in and help you. Admit your need now.

I'm warm. I'm sure of it. And it matters little. The battle is too great. I'm overwhelmed. Lost. It's up to God alone now. I sleep.

Deep breathe in...and out.

I awaken hours later, stiff and cold but breathing. I test out each leg, moving the left, then the right. Each arm. I wiggle my toes and fingers.

Feel yourself testing your body from neck to toe.

I'm alive. I laugh under my breath. Unbelievable, really. It's early morning, judging by the pink light filtering through my snow-packed walls. God has seen me through!

I take a drink from my nearly frozen canteen, feeling the icy liquid move past my teeth, down my throat. It's time to see my way out. Maybe there'll be a rescue team searching for me. I wiggle out of my tight spot, realizing it could've been my tomb, and kick out one wall. I crawl out and put on my snowshoes. Then I rise and pull on my backpack.

But I halt with only one arm through a strap. And then I laugh out loud. It starts as a giggle and ends in a laugh that shakes my entire body.

Because I'm in my meadow—my original destination! All around me are sharp cliff faces, carved from the ice and wind of several millenniums' work. Clean, glistening snow surrounds me, covers the trees. It's the most beautiful spot in the world.

See yourself there, admiring the pristine, gorgeous surroundings. Thank the Father for seeing you through this battle, for saving you.

"Lord, You've been so good to me," I whisper. "Thank You. Thank You."

Consider how He's seen you through this, how He can see you through anything. No matter what the conflict, no matter what the battle, no matter who the enemy. He will see you through. Deep breathe in…and out.

He will see me through. Now that I know where I am, I can clearly see my path back. A red-and-white helicopter roars overhead, then turns in a broad circle, spotting me.

I shake my head in wonder at God's power, the wonder of His care and shelter. *He will see me through.* Through it all. No matter what, no matter where. Somehow.

He'll see me through.

He is the conqueror.

He will see you through.

Amen. ⨝

Chapter Nine

OASIS

WHEN YOU NEED FORGIVENESS

God is grace.

NEHEMIAH 9:17; MARK 11:25

Be still before the Lord: Sit down in a chair with your shoes off, feet spread comfortably apart, hands on thighs. Close your eyes and take three deep breaths, in and out. Lift your pinky toe, trying not to move the others. Don't make it a tense exercise, just an exercise in understanding. Now try your big toe. Notice how moving one seems to move the others.

Now try one of your fingers (not your thumb). See how much easier that is? But it still moves the others too, right?

Consider for a moment how one movement sets off another; how another movement leaves the rest alone, quiet, still.

Think about sin. In your own life. How one movement sets off a whole cascade of other movement. How it seems to take on a life of its own, once that first sorry decision is made.

Deep breathe in...and out.

Read and reflect: What does "stiff-necked" mean? In the Bible, it refers to those who are arrogant and refuse to obey the rules, rebelling against God's laws. As we make our way through our crazy lives, doesn't the tension build in our necks and shoulders? Don't we become so burdened and busy that we find it hard to get back to the One who can alleviate much of our stress and sorrows? Spending routine time with the Savior can lower our blood pressure, improve our health, and give us hope for our future.

Regardless of what has transpired, regardless of how we've walked away from the light and into the darkness, God is still a "forgiving God, gracious and compassionate, slow to anger and abounding in love"; because of His "great compassion," He doesn't "abandon [us] in the desert" (Nehemiah 9:17,19).

Enter into prayer: Pause periodically to focus on your senses, bringing the scene described below to life. Use the ends of paragraphs to stop and consider sight, smell, sound, and touch. Read each sentence slowly, pausing often to dwell upon the meaning for you.

Take a deep, slow breath. In and out, in and out.

Father, take this tension from my shoulders, my neck, my heart, my life. Help me to see all the ways that sin is impacting me and impeding me, and help me to confess. As I pray, bring me into Your light and away from the prince of darkness. In Jesus' name, Amen.

DESERT SAND. I HAVEN'T SEEN this much sand ever. In all my life. It surrounds me...for miles and miles it surrounds me.

Imagine yourself in the midst of a massive desert, nothing but crusty sand everywhere you look. See yourself doing a slow three-sixty, understanding that the road home is nowhere near, that your reserves are few.

I know my name, my age, my address, but for the life of me, I can't remember how I got here. When I raise my hand to my brow, wiping it of sweat, I wonder if my wrist is sprained. My fingers run over a gritty crust on my forehead, and when I lower my hand, dried blood is visible upon them. Was I in a car accident?

It matters little. I turn again and find that my footprints behind me are washed away in the blowing sand. I trudge up a steep incline and pause, searching the arid horizon again. By the sun, I'd guess that it's midmorning.

Imagine a full day of desert heat before you.

My only chance is to keep moving.

Feeling the sun beating down on my scalp, the distinctive burning sensation of solar heat on flesh, I untie the sweatshirt from about my waist and cover my head. It alleviates the immediate pain, but I suffer with the added heat of the cloth. It feels heavy, more like carrying a crate or a jug of water than a mere sweatshirt. If only it were water...

Since I have no idea what happened, why I'm here, there's little way for me to discern why I would set off without any water, why I wouldn't keep to any road. It seems crazy, foolish. Uneasily, I wonder if I meant to kill myself. Maybe I have amnesia.

But I remember, I remember everything else. If only I could forget it! The things that surface to my mind are not mundane things like a to-do list or my schedule, but the things that have burdened me for months, for years. The things that threaten to dry me out, to kill me, like this desert before me.

Take a moment to consider the deathly, burdening things in your own life. How has sin impacted you? What is it doing to you now? Don't confess it yet. Ruminate on the power of it, the sheer stark blackness of it. Can you almost see it as a tangible force crowding out God's light in your heart?

It strikes me then: Maybe God brought me here. He's brought me so far, done so much for me, but again and again I've turned a cold shoulder His way. Maybe He sees me as He did His people in the desert after He brought them out of Egypt—sculpting golden cows to worship instead of the God who saves.

Name the golden cows you've worshiped. Power. Riches. Control. Pride. What? Name them.

Deep breathe in...and out.

Name any other sin that binds you. Anything that comes to mind.
From today, yesterday, last year, decades ago. Name them now.

I stumble forward, naming my sins, acknowledging them, feeling their weight upon my shoulders. It's like they've been there forever, lurking, stalking, just waiting to move forward, to surround me, suffocate me—yet they seem to emerge from inside me, not from the outside.

I pause in my walk, paradoxically lost in the darkness even while the brightest sun I've ever witnessed beats down upon me. I'm so engulfed by the complex fabric of my sin and my shame that I have trouble breathing.

"Help," I mutter heavenward. "Help. Help me. Help!"

"Breathe," comes the answer. "Breathe and walk. Breathe."

Deep breathe in...and out. In...and out.

I do as He asks, trembling before Him. I don't see Him. But He is here. And the idea of it brings me to my knees. "I'm sorry, Lord. So sorry. Forgive me, forgive me, forgive me."

Silently repeat your petition for forgiveness now.

The wind beats at my back, flowing past me, pulling at me. I hear Him calling to me again. "Walk. Rise and walk. Come."

As I rise, the wind gentles to a breeze, feeling more like the brush of angels' wings than of earthly elements. This makes sense—*He* is here. He's urging me forward. To safety? To forgiveness? To life?

The weight of my sin has lessened with my confession, but I still feel it, like a light shawl about my shoulders, ready to become lead at any given moment. It holds me hostage, this vestige of sin.

"It is not I who leaves it there," He says to my heart. "It is you. Accept My forgiveness, child. Come."

I do as He asks, trudging over sand dune after sand dune after sand dune. Will my path never end? My tongue feels thick in my dry mouth, my lips are splitting. I squint in the bright sunlight. My one reprieve is that I no longer sweat, but somewhere within me, I understand that that's a bad thing. I'm dehydrated. Dangerously so.

"Lord—"

Water. He knows what I need. He simply calls me forward.

Of course He knows. I feel dizzy, lightheaded, suddenly giddy and silly. He formed me in my mother's womb, made sure to make me who I am, because He loved me even then. Of course He knows I need water. He knows everything I need.

But still. "I need it now, Father. I need—"

I pause on the crest of yet another dune. In the distance, dancing in the heat waves hovering over the acres before me, is a palm tree.

No. It can't be. Yes. It is.

A palm tree can only mean water.

Consider the joy of such a vision. The relief, the hope as it floods your heart. You stumble forward, fall, pick yourself up and stumble forward again. See yourself there. Feel the sand on your hands, on your face, but also the impossible hope before you.

As I get closer, I hear it. Pounding, rushing, pulsing, dripping, beating, singing...water. I lick my lips in anticipation, but there's no moisture on my tongue.

My eyes search the cacophony of green before me, the mad jungle rush of foliage in comparison to the dry desert behind. It's almost too much to take in, to acknowledge.

It's an oasis.

"Come," my Savior calls. "Walk, crawl, skip, run. Come."

I push past spare green plants on the outside edge of the oasis, guardians for the more lush plants of the interior. As the palm branches close in above me, I rush toward the center of my desert paradise, intent on finding the water, the water, the water.

Five steps, ten steps more, and I'm there, suddenly milling my arms backward in an instinctual effort to keep from falling, then laughing, giving up, and falling into the cool pool before me. Two feet of water breaks my fall, then my hands meet the sandy bottom. One taste and I know this is fresh water that meets my lips.

I rise from the shallows, gasp for air, then drink and drink.

See yourself there, on your knees, cupping your hands to drink.

At last, I thirst no longer.

Feel the luxury of it—something you desperately needed is finally so readily available. Feel the end of thirst.

The pool—an impossible blue—is perhaps twenty feet across, bubbling up from a spring on the far end, surrounded by lush plants. I stand and can easily see there's nothing but sand in the clear depths.

"Thank You, Father," I whisper, wiping my dripping face, relishing the feel of moisture upon my parched lips.

Silently thank Him now.

But still I feel the mantle of my past shame clinging to me as surely as my wet clothes.

"Come," He calls. "Come."

Instinctively, I crouch and push toward deeper water, feeling the cool liquid surround me. I turn to float on my back and gaze upward to the palm branches fluttering in the desert breeze high above me, a comforting green canopy against the sun. I reach the center of the pool and float on the calm waters.

Then I'm still, the sounds of my own breathing loud in my own ears.

Deep breathe in...and out.

He's whispering to me.

"Let Me cleanse you. Let Me free you. Accept My forgiveness. Feel it wash away your mantle of shame forever. Accept it, child of Mine. Accept it. Appreciate it, but accept it. Do not bear your burden any longer. Relinquish it to Me. It's why I came. For you. It's why I bore the cross. For you."

The thought of Him upon the cross brings tears to my eyes. I feel my burden of guilt. "No, Lord. No."

"You must. If you do not accept the gift, it negates the gift."

I swallow hard against the lump in my throat.

A gift. A man's life. God's life. For my own.

I'm humbled. And yet I'm also hollow. Without this gift, I will forever be burdened.

"Take it," He says. I hear Him call my name.

Hear your name upon His lips.

"Take it from Me. I give you this gift because I love you, so that you might forever be pardoned. Take it."

I take a deep breath and fold my hands above me, sinking into the cool depths, feeling the water close over me. It feels as if I am encapsulated by the Spirit, enveloped by God Himself.

"Wash me," I pray silently.

Silently repeat the prayer.

"Cleanse me."

Repeat.

"Heal me."

Repeat.

As I rise to the surface again, the water pulls and pulls and pulls at the tendrils of sin that I cling to. They aren't clinging to me; it is I that hold on to them, not fully accepting God's forgiveness, whether I wallow or dip in the shame of my past.

This time I let them go, and I breathe and breathe and breathe, feeling like I've never before taken such deep, lusty lungfuls in all my life.

Feel the liberation, the freedom of this moment.
Feel your lungs expand outward against your chest walls.
Embrace the space, the luxury.

As I swim to the edge of the pool, I want to tell others of this independence, this peace, this breathing room, all found within the confines of the oasis.

It's then that I understand: In living the gift, I honor the gift. And in honoring the gift, I fully accept the gift. And in accepting the gift, I please my Lord.

I make my way out of the oasis, intent on finding my way home. I'm already mostly there. And no desert can harm me.

Amen. ✍

Chapter Ten

KNOWN AND LOVED

WHEN YOU FEEL ORPHANED BY LIFE

God is love.

DEUTERONOMY 33:12

Be still before the Lord: Chanting is an ancient Christian practice that incorporates the entire body and forces one to think more clearly of the words one is speaking. Try chanting a psalm. (Quit laughing; you can do it.) Concentrate on the fact that you're one of millions throughout thousands of years of history who have lifted these words to God. Don't you think it would please Him to hear you join in?

Get to someplace quiet and secluded, where you won't think about anyone hearing you but God. It can be in the middle of a forest, in the privacy of your room, or in your car. Take three deep, slow breaths.

Now thoughtfully try your hand at chanting, slowly lifting to the Lord the words printed below from Psalm 121. Keeping your voice quiet and monotone, lift a note or two at the end of the first sentence, then drop a note or two at the end of the second. (God doesn't care if your voice is worthy of a recording contract or sadly off-key. He loves you. He loves your voice. He created it just as it is. This is a sacrifice of praise.)

> I lift up my eyes to the hills—
> where does my help come from?

My help comes from the LORD,
    the Maker of heaven and earth.
He will not let your foot slip—
    he who watches over you will not slumber;
indeed, he who watches over Israel
    will neither slumber nor sleep.
The LORD watches over you—
    the LORD is your shade at your right hand;
the sun will not harm you by day,
    nor the moon by night.
The LORD will keep you from all harm—
    he will watch over your life;
the LORD will watch over your coming
        and going
    both now and forevermore.

Read and reflect: Now silently read over those words from Psalm 121 again, hearing your voice as one with thousands of others in stately, reverent praise. Pause after each verse, listening to the notes in your mind as they hang in the air while you reflect.

What does it mean to look "to the hills"? What does it mean to be watched over by an unsleeping guardian—One who watches over all His faithful? What does it mean to have constant "shade at your right hand"—protection from anything that threatens during the day or during the night?

What does it mean to have Him watching "over your coming and going both now and forevermore"?

Enter into prayer: *Lord God, as I think about being known and loved, help me to focus on You through Christ. With the fire of Your light, keep the evil prowling lion away. In Jesus' name. Amen.*

THE SHADOWS of the towering buildings engulf me. When I look up at their sleek sides—fifty, eighty, a hundred stories tall—they seem to veer away. I know it's an optical illusion, but I wonder if even the buildings want nothing to do with me.

It makes me slightly dizzy to stare up at such great heights, so I return my eyes to the cracked sidewalk and continue on my journey.

I've wandered the city streets for hours, feeling shell-shocked and lost. Everything looks the same; nothing feels familiar. I'm in a maze of concrete and asphalt and glass and metal. A few trees along the boulevard struggle to find their way to live, enduring the taxi cab exhaust and the sheltered light. A few planters at hotel entrances pretend to be thriving, but I know new flowers must be transplanted there weekly.

Right foot, left foot, right foot, left. I walk and walk and walk.

I'm out of a job, let go, as of a week ago.

> *See your feet before you as you walk.*
> *Right foot, left foot, right foot, left.*

I have no one significant to love.

> *Right foot, left foot, right foot, left.*

I have but a few days in my apartment remaining before I'm kicked out.

> *Right foot, left foot, right foot, left.*

I have no money for food.

> *Right foot, left foot, right foot, left.*

No family on this side of the seaboard. What am I to do?

> *Have you ever reached the end of your rope? Wondered how*
> *in the world you were going to survive the coming week? Unable*
> *to think of much beyond each step before you, one at a time?*
> *Take a moment to recall a moment when you felt orphaned by life,*
> *lost, in pain, alone. Maybe it's now; maybe it was twenty years ago.*

The shadows are lengthening on the streets; the buildings are like great sundials telling me that evening approaches. Still, I can't find it in me to go home. My tiny, old apartment with its cardboard walls and peeling paint has never felt like home. I will find no comfort there.

A commuter train, high on its tracks, rumbles by me, creating a thundering echo in my chest. Nameless faces stare out of the train windows at me, not seeing me, not really.

No one sees me anymore. They've called me by name; they've put paper on my desk and removed paper from my trash bin; they've made small talk with me at the water cooler or the apartment mailbox; but no one really knows me.

I loved—once. But my love was taken in hand and squeezed so tightly that it disappeared into a handful of dust particles. With one breath, those particles disappeared on the wind. And my lover disappeared as well.

So now I walk, walk, walk. Watching my feet, finding a surreal satisfaction in their distant workings when nothing else in my life is on track.

Right foot, left foot, right foot, left.

Then I lift my eyes to the street and watch as office hours come to a close and workers flood from their gates. Just as I did, until a week ago.

I stand in the middle of the sidewalk, staring forward. The sea of people parts before me; they walk around me as if I'm a lamppost or a fire hydrant. Few look me in the eye. Those who do quickly look away.

What do they see in me, in my eyes? Fear? Sorrow? Anxiety? Desperation?

I'm alone. Orphaned. Amid so many people, I walk alone.

"Where are You, Father?" I mutter, staring at my feet again, gaining strength from their endurance. How many miles have I covered today, walking down Hyatt and up Ninth Avenue and down Broadway and up Sixteenth? I've gone from the baseball stadium to the freeway and back again. I've walked under the commuter train tracks five times. All day I've walked this trek, looking, looking, looking. Wandering. Seeking. Seeking what?

In this situation, what would you be looking for? Searching for?

"Where are You, Jesus?" I ask. I lift my eyes to the crowd. A few people hear me. They mutter disparaging things or merely frown and look away. No one wants to hear me, touch me, see me. Has even God abandoned me?

A large man bumps my shoulder, and I career right, away from the street. Then directly before me a bum in dirty pants, legs outstretched, forces me to hurtle myself across the crevasse of his legs. I don't quite make it. Stumbling, falling, crashing to the cement with a cry of fear, a grunt of impact, a moan of pain spreading through my body.

The bum pats my calves. "Say, friend, you all right?"

"No," I pause, trying to gain a breath. "No, I'm not all right."

See yourself there. Feel yourself recoiling at the man's touch. Measure the pain in your body, in your soul, from impact. From life.

He's watching me curl into a ball beside him, fighting for breath, trying to gain my sea legs again to rise.

I can feel his gaze upon me. But I cannot yet muster the breath needed to move, to move away.

"You break anything?" he asks.

"No." I say, thinking about my aching elbows. Then I get to thinking about my heart and soul and entire *life*. "And yes," I add.

"What's that? You hurt?"

I finally have enough breath to rise to a sitting position. I lean against the brick wall, as the man does, and I close my eyes.

"Need a doctor?"

"If he can fix my life."

It's bad, really bad. I know my life's a disaster when I have to sit next to a bum on the street to get someone to listen to me.

He answers, "Only one doctor who can fix a life."

I chance a glance at him. He's a young man, though well worn. Missing teeth, dirty clothes that stink of urine and body odor and city streets.

"Who's that?"

"That's what we're all trying to figure out now, isn't it? Got a dollar?"

I laugh under my breath, though there's no humor in it. I stare at the crowd, now dwindling, like a tidal wave that, once past, has only small waves behind it. None of the people look at us, even when my new companion reaches out with his tattered basket and asks for spare change.

I don't know why I don't immediately move away. There's something about him that draws me, holds me.

See yourself there, sitting beside the young man.

"You think life is a series of trials?" I ask.

"Had my share," he says.

"Tell me."

He looks at me, really looks at me, and I think again how desperate I must be to appreciate even a perfect stranger's moment of bonding. His dark brown eyes show a measure of fear and curiosity mixed together. He decides to trust me a little.

"First there was my mama, who died when I was five. Then there was my daddy, who beat me until I was nine. Then I hit the streets and made my own way until I got a disease in my leg bones. Now I can barely walk."

I sit back and stare ahead for a while, thinking that my pain pales in comparison. I glance at him again. "How can you smile anymore, talk...live?"

He stares at me, and a measure of love and empathy enters his eyes. I stare back, transfixed. No one has looked at me like this in some time. "Somebody told me once that you can either be sorry the rosebush has thorns, or be glad the thornbush has roses. Either way, you keep going. But some-times you gotta focus on those roses."

Consider that phrase. What does it mean to see the rosebush
with thorns versus the thornbush with roses?

I nod, slowly, thinking on that. "What if you can't see the roses?"

"Oh, there's always roses. Might be just a few petals cling-ing to an old bud or a green bud ready to burst. But there's always roses." His smile is sudden and wide and contagious.

I lean back, as if feeling the force of it. Who is this man? After a moment, I rise to leave.

"Got a dollar?" he asks.

I laugh again, under my breath, and dig deep into my pocket. "I have three."

"Well, you seem down on your luck. How about you keep two and give me one?"

I smile and nod, handing him a crumpled green bill. I start to say good-bye, to leave for my apartment, but I'm troubled at the thought of leaving him here. "Got someplace to spend the night?"

"I do. There's a shelter around the corner. A buddy comes and helps me there."

I nod, still not satisfied. What is it about his eyes, those almost black eyes, that keep drawing me?

"Got a coat?" I ask. I remember an old one of my father's hanging in my closet. "I could get you one."

He smiles. Again I feel a wave of warmth wash through me. Comfort. Peace. Joy.

> *Feel it wash through you. What does sheer pleasure, sheer joy, sheer gladness feel like? Feel it wash through you now, like a wave.*

I take a chance and introduce myself.

> *See yourself lean down and take the man's hand in yours and shake it, thinking not of germs or dirt, but of the peace—the sheer astonishing peace—in this man's eyes.*

"Pleasure to meet you," he says again. He shakes and shakes and shakes my hand, and I sense there's old knowledge in his eyes. Ancient knowledge.

> *Hear your name coming from his lips. Feel the strength in his hand and wrist, the friendly grip, the genuine warmth in his friendly shake. The knowing of you, from inside out. The acceptance.*

"I have a word for you before you leave," he says.

"What's that?"

"You are known. You are loved."

I stare at him. There's no way he could know what I've gone through, where I've been, what has happened to me. Is there?

A verse pops into my head, unbidden: *I tell you the truth, whatever you did for one of the least of these brothers of mine, you did for me.*

I stare back at my new friend, transfixed by the truth that shines from his eyes. The knowledge, the peace, the understanding, the promise.

Consider for a moment what truth and promise would look like in this man's eyes. God's purest peace. Holy understanding.

There's no way he could know. Is there?

"You go on now," he tells me. "Keep walking. One foot after the other. But remember to look for the roses. And that you are known and loved. You are not forgotten. *You are not forgotten.*"

I smile, and my smile seems to use muscles that have atrophied. But they work. Somehow, they still work.

I pull out my last two dollars and fold his fingers around them. I'll find my way without them. To a new job, a new apartment, a new life.

Because I'm already surrounded by this reminder of an old, old love. A love I have known all of my days.

I turn and walk again.

Right foot, left foot, right foot, left.

At the corner, I turn to wave at the man on the sidewalk, one last farewell.

But he's gone.

And in his place is one perfect red rose.

Father God, help me to remember that even when I feel most lost, most orphaned by life, You haven't abandoned me, You'll never abandon me. Give me the courage to cling to hope, to look for the roses among the thorns, to see where You're leading me next.

Most of all, Lord, help me to remember that I'm never ever totally alone. Amen.

Chapter Eleven

❧

FREEDOM

WHEN YOU NEED A SAVIOR

God is merciful.

ISAIAH 45:22

꙰

Be still before the Lord: Find a chair in a quiet, isolated part of the house. Get a pillow to place behind your lower back if you don't have good support. Your feet should be shoulder-width apart, hands on thighs, shoulders rolled back and dropped.

Take three slow, deep breaths. Then consider how God made every inch of you. Think about this, beginning at the tips of your toes and moving up through your legs, through your torso, up through your neck and head, all the way to the tips of your hair strands. Take three minutes to do this, then go back and start again. Slowly, slowly, see yourself as a fine craft of the Lord's. Flaws and all, you belong to Him.

When you're finished, take three more deep, slow breaths.

Read and reflect: Ephesians 2 (in *The Message*) tells us,

> You let the world, which doesn't know the
> first thing about living, tell you how to live.
> You filled your lungs with polluted unbelief,
> and then exhaled disobedience. We all did it,
> all of us doing what we felt like doing, when

we felt like doing it, all of us in the same boat. It's a wonder God didn't lose his temper and do away with the whole lot of us. Instead, immense in mercy and with an incredible love, he embraced us. He took our sin-dead lives and made us alive in Christ. He did all this on his own, with no help from us!...

Saving is all his idea, and all his work. All we do is trust him enough to let him do it. It's God's gift from start to finish!... No, we neither make nor save ourselves. God does both the making and saving.

Repeat each of the following phrases silently, hearing them echoing forward as if you're speaking in an empty auditorium with great acoustics: *God loves me. God made me. God saved me. I accept Christ's gift to me. By grace I am saved.*

Do this again and again until you feel the words in your heart as truth.

Enter into prayer: *Father in heaven, as I enter into this time of stillness and reflection, please bless me with clarity of thought and image. Keep the Evil One at bay, and keep my thoughts solely on You and Yours. Help me see how I need you as my Savior each and every day. In Jesus' name. Amen.*

IT'S NOT THE KIND of chill to be overcome by slipping on a sweater, but rather a chill that emanates from the marrow of my bones.

"Empty your pockets," the prison guard lackadaisically demands, gesturing toward the plastic box on the shelf before me.

I don't have much, but the guard wearily writes down the contents on a triplicate form, then hands me a Bic pen. "Sign at the bottom."

Distantly I agree that it's all I have, all I have left, and dutifully sign on the bottom line, remembering the Mont Blanc pen I loved and left behind. It was part of my former life, when I was whole. Now I'm half the person I used to be. The pen had gone perfectly with my high-rise office downtown, with its antique mahogany furniture and lush carpets and a secretary at my beck and call. But all that is no more. I am no more.

Another guard slaps a lid onto the plastic box, labeling it with my last name and a number, my prisoner ID.

How can this be possible? None of this seems real to me yet. But it's real, all right. Too real.

I glance backward, even as I hear the metallic door ahead of me clicking open. I want to keep my eyes on that box, because it represents the last vestiges of my former life, the last symbols of all I held true and good. But it's gone, already neatly filed away as I am about to be neatly filed away.

"Come on," the guard says in irritation, pulling me forward. In the next room I strip before an impassive guard and take a shower. Then I'm taken, shivering, to a doctor to be examined.

Film clips of other lost lives flit through my head. I'm dehumanized. A number. Another prisoner to track and manage. There's no care, no deference in this world for another human being. Only the process.

The doctor signs off on my good health with a grunt. On a table beside me he tosses a stiff orange jumpsuit of rough cotton, underwear, and prison-issue shoes. There's no meager curtain for privacy. Privacy is gone with the other luxuries of a citizen's life.

I'm a criminal.

> *Take a moment to consider yourself in this prisoner's shoes.*
> *Stripped of your family, your friends, your home, your career,*
> *your possessions. Everything you love. See yourself there.*
> *What would it feel like? What happens to dignity? Pride?*

I want to close my eyes and open them, to make this nightmare go away. From the time the judge pounded his gavel, the sound echoing through my ears in dreamlike fashion, nothing has seemed right. It's all wrong, wrong, wrong.

I laugh at myself. But it's right. This is justice. I've been sentenced for my sins. This is where I belong. My loved ones wailed and cried as I was led from the courtroom. I wanted to scream that I was innocent, but in my heart I knew. This was what I deserved. This was fitting punishment.

I'm a criminal.

What are you guilty of? What sins have you committed? Name them all now.

The guard and I move through another metal gate whose clanging jars me like fingernails on a chalkboard. Inside, from their cells, the other prisoners stare at me, shouting profanities and catcalls.

What would these other prisoners call you? How would they bait you? See yourself there.

I try to swallow, but my throat is dry and tight. I cough instead, a brittle, wheezing sound. My mind runs wild, considering what it will be like to face these other prisoners in the yard, in the dining hall.

Who will protect you? Will you want their protection? What will be the price?

It doesn't take long to deduce that the "outside" is a whole different world from the "inside." I'm not tough. I don't know if I'll have the strength to make it through this with my sanity and my body intact. Everything in me tells me to flee, to get out of here, but the shackles at my feet and the bars at the door would make it a short flight.

Forcing myself to breathe slowly, I keep my eyes looking straight ahead, the inmates' filthy words making my skin crawl. The guard leads me up three flights of stairs and down an iron walkway, then pulls me to a stop. The closest I'd ever been before to a prison was in Hollywood movies. Now he unlocks the cell door and mocks me with a gesture of invitation. Head held high and stiff, I enter.

I barely clear the doorway when the bars toll with a funereal sound behind me, making me wince. A shout rises up from the other inmates in neighboring cells, as if cheered that I've joined their ranks.

In your head, hear this uproar of communal misery.

As their cries fade, the diversion over, I look about my ten-by-five-foot cell. A metal toilet with no seat. A bare sink. A sorry looking cot with one blanket. Peach walls—to keep us calm, I acknowledge. I'm doomed to years of peach and metal.

I shiver. I pull the blanket from the bed, wrap it around my shoulders, then sit down on the cot, its coils creaking under my weight.

I tuck my knees against my chest and lean backward into the corner of the cell, ignoring the calls of the inmates on either side of me. I feel like a cornered fox in a cave with hunters all about, dogs at the entrance. Trapped.

I stay in that position—an hour, maybe two?—until my bladder insists I do something about it. Knowing I'm foolish, that modesty is a luxury already long gone, I keep the blanket wrapped around me while I use the toilet. There's no soap at the sink as I wash up. I stare at my hands, icy water running over them, as if they belong to someone else.

For the first time, staring into the shiny metal that passes as a mirror, I mutter a prayer. "Dear God, what have I done?"

> *Begin to acknowledge your sins to God,*
> *to confess them by admitting them to yourself.*

There's no answer. I expect none.

I'm a criminal.

I climb back into my corner and wrap the blanket more tightly around my shoulders. I nod off to sleep, huddled in that position...

The morning guard awakens me by running a wooden baton across the metal bars, and he adds a ridiculing joke. His laugh echoes down the cellblock. The prisoners pretty much ignore him. Maybe he says the same thing every day.

I unfold my stiff legs and groan as I get to my feet. I'll be a model prisoner. They'll let me out for good behavior. My crime is white-collar. They don't keep people in prison for twenty-year sentences for white-collar crimes. No way. I just have to keep my nose clean, steer clear of trouble.

But trouble aims for me these days.

In the cafeteria, after I receive my tray with orange juice and oatmeal and runny eggs, I can feel the other prisoners' eyes on me, the new arrival.

I walk to my table but stumble over someone's out-stretched foot. I come down hard, the breath knocked out of me, my breakfast flying forward, landing all over two menacing prisoners.

A guard yanks me to my feet and ushers me quickly away, but not before the inmates turn to face me. Two new enemies. I groan.

> *Acknowledge your world getting*
> *just a little darker when it's already dark.*

"You're in for it now," the guard says.

"Someone tripped me."

"In here, you can't plead innocent anymore," he sneers.

> *Another guard takes my other arm,*
> *and they lead me to my cell. Standard practice, I can tell.*
> *Remove the pigeon food before all the pigeons descend.*

"I need a drink," I say, as they shut my door and walk away.

"There's water in the sink," the guard tosses over his shoulder.

My stomach rumbles in hunger, and I sit down on the edge of the cot. I miss my refrigerator and my table, my family and my home. For the first time, the impact of my sentence hits me. I'm not returning home. I'm not going to embrace my family or see much of my friends or be in my own home for years.

For years. I sit and contemplate this for a full minute.

> *Think about not going home for years. Of being separated*
> *from family and friends and all you hold dear.*

"O God," I say under my breath, emitting my second prayer since arriving. "I'm sorry. I'm so sorry." I pull the blanket from the cot and wrap it around my shoulders again. But there's no warding off a chill that begins inside.

In the days that follow, my life settles into the rhythm of the prison. The meals, the exercise yard, the mindless assembly-line work. Dodging scuffles, evading arguments, but still getting someone's fist to my belly on occasion. Before this, I'd never known what it felt like to be hit. My battles had been verbal, mental, never physical.

The library cart becomes my sustenance, the thing that keeps me sane, my temporary escape from my dark, dark world. That—and Sunday services.

The chaplain is a kind man, silver-haired but ageless in countenance. His name is Rupert, and his skin is as ebony black as his tightly coiled hair is white. His eyes are frequently bloodshot, as if he stays up all night. Maybe he does, praying for the salvation of his ragtag flock, but he always makes me feel he has all the time in the world for me, that I'm the most important person on Cellblock K. And I know I'm not the only one who feels that way.

See yourself in prison for days...and weeks...and months...and years. Getting used to this new life. Clinging to new hope. Evading danger. Making alliances. Coping. Take a deep breath in...and out.

Through the years Pastor Rupert and I have become closer and closer. He has helped me to see the error of my thinking, my way of explaining away gray things that ultimately caught up with me. But I still haven't fully confessed my sins and asked Jesus to help me. I just can't get to that place. But Rupert's working on me, hard. He knows as well as I do that the parole board is meeting in a month. He knows it weakens my resolve to hold in my sin.

Today, sitting in the tiny prison chapel, Rupert puts his hand on my shoulder and says my name with such love and understanding that I want to weep. Nobody inside speaks to a prisoner the same way Pastor Rupert does.

Hear your name from this man with utter love and understanding in his voice. There's nothing you could do or say that would push him away.

He's explaining the situation: "The parole board doesn't want you to say the words they want to hear. They want to hear the words your heart longs to say. To get that clear, you first gotta say those words to God, to your Savior, Jesus Christ. You understand?"

I nod, not totally comprehending, but hearing it, all right. He hands me his old, worn Bible, open to the place he wants me to read, then leaves me in the chapel.

Although I know there's a guard outside, I revel in the relative feeling of freedom. In five long years inside, I've never had the intimacy and quiet that the small, cheap chapel affords me now. The pews are undoubtedly hand-me-downs from a forgotten country church; the walls are windowless. The altar table and cross up front are of plain pine, unadorned with artwork or carving or linens. But to me, it's heaven.

I glance down at the Bible in my hands and focus on the words from Ephesians: "But because of his great love for us, God, who is rich in mercy, made us alive with Christ even when we were dead in transgressions—it is by grace you have been saved...through faith—and this not from yourselves, it is the gift of God—not by works."

I swallow hard, rise, then slowly approach the altar.

I'm a criminal.

Rich in mercy.

I'm a criminal.

Dead in transgressions.

I'm a criminal.

By grace you have been saved.

I'm a criminal.

By grace, saved, a gift of God.

My mind circles back to Rupert, to what he said. *The words your heart longs to say.* What does my heart long to say?

What does your heart long to say?

My years inside have toughened me, inside and out. There was no choice. *Get stronger or die* is a prisoner's motto.

Rupert's words speak to a cry deep within me, a longing for something more, something else, something free. Do I dare hope? Do I dare to tell my God all that I crave?

Do you dare?

He's certainly safer than my cellblock neighbors. But as I kneel before that plain wooden cross and altar, I know I'm no more innocent than the other inmates. My crimes, though white-collar, had hurt countless people. People were out of work because of me. Families lost their homes. Marriages split apart. Children without parents. And *not* because of a mistake. Because of my wrongdoing. Because of my sin.

I'm a criminal.

I can't save myself from this place. I can't land a get-out-of-jail-free card from Rupert. My punishment will extend beyond the prison walls anyway. I'll forever deal with this loneliness, this culpability, this distancing, this sin.

I weep for the first time. The cistern overflows. It has been long in coming, this grief pouring.

As you confess, feel the guilt, the anguish, the pain, and the fear release from you like a container of water broken open, flowing outward.

"Dear God," I say through my tears. "Dear God! Hear me!"

Call out to Him.

"Lord, I'm a sinner. Forgive me. Please forgive me. Help the people I've wronged to forgive me."

Ask His forgiveness now.

I sink to the concrete steps, hearing my pitiful cries echo outward, making me weep all the more. For the first time, I feel the depths of my mistakes, my sins, my depravity, my loneliness. The chill of my distance from the Savior.

Acknowledge the depths now.

"Father in heaven, I need a Savior. I need You. Please forgive me. Take my burdens upon You. Help me to lean upon You. I need You. I need You. I need You. Only by Your grace am I saved."

Ask Him into your heart. Tell Him of your need.
For Him and Him alone.

I cry for several minutes longer, emptying the garbage that pollutes my soul. Right here on the chapel steps, stretched out over three steps, shaking as I sob through it all, through all the sorrow and misery, I empty myself and allow my Savior to take on my burdens at last.

After a while, my weeping abates. I'm empty, weary. And feeling curiously clean. The empty feeling fades, and in its place is a cloudy filling I can't quite get my hands around, but I accept it. Gratefully, I accept it.

I'm a criminal. But by grace, I'm saved.

Accept God's filling of peace in you now.
Thank Him for taking on your burdens, for being your Savior.

Rupert enters quietly and lays a hand on my shoulder. "Amen," he says. He sits down beside me, opens his arms in invitation, and holds me for a long moment.

At last I pull away and wipe my eyes, smiling through the remnants of my tears. "I didn't know. I didn't know I hadn't bared it all to God. I didn't know there was more in my heart."

"There's always more in our hearts," he says kindly. "That's why we need Jesus."

I stare at my friend, knowing he speaks the truth. Knowing his words have the light of the Father in them. And I also know that I've taken the very first step—the first of many—toward true freedom.

Amen. ⚔

Chapter Twelve

THE GLORY
OF A NIGHT SKY

WHEN YOU'RE FILLED
WITH AWE BY HIS CREATIVITY

God is majestic.

JOB 37:22-24

Be still before the Lord: Gather pen and paper. Quickly write out all that comes to mind under two headings: Details and Big Stuff. (For example: "Make a dental appointment" for Details; "Apologize to my spouse" for Big Stuff.) Take five minutes to empty your brain of all the things that crowd it, keeping you from quiet, uninterrupted time with God.

Then fold the paper, place it in an envelope, write "To God" on the outside, and commit to Him both this time and all that follows it—when you can go after the details and the big stuff. He'll walk you through all of it. Place the envelope in a safe place, somewhere you can turn to later.

Now that it's all written down, you can move on to bigger things. Like the amazing wonder of God and His creation.

Follow this exercise with two minutes of deeper, more dramatic breathing. Completely fill your lungs, completely empty them, then simply allow yourself deep, relaxed breathing.

Read and reflect: Who can express God's majesty better than David in Psalm 8? Consider this paraphrase by Eugene Peterson in *The Message,* pausing over each phrase to fully comprehend the wonder and understanding in the psalmist's words:

> GOD, brilliant Lord,
>   yours is a household name.
> Nursing infants gurgle choruses about you;
>   toddlers shout the songs
> That drown out enemy talk,
>   and silence atheist babble.
> I look up at your macro-skies, dark
>   and enormous,
>   your handmade sky-jewelry,
> Moon and stars mounted in their settings.
>   Then I look at my micro-self and wonder,
> Why do you bother with us?
>   Why take a second look our way?
> Yet we've so narrowly missed being gods,
>   bright with Eden's dawn light.
> You put us in charge of your handcrafted world,
>   repeated to us your Genesis-charge,
> Made us lords of sheep and cattle,
>   even animals out in the wild,
> Birds flying and fish swimming,
>   whales singing in the ocean deeps.
> God, brilliant Lord,
>   your name echoes around the world.

Enter into prayer: *Father God, as I consider the wonder of Your creation, the breadth and width of Your movement in our world, keep my eyes focused on You and not on the Evil One. Sanctify my imagination and use this prayer to draw me closer to You alone. In Jesus' name. Amen.*

IT'S QUIET on the lake, blissfully quiet. I take a deep breath and acknowledge the scents of water and decomposing plants and the faintest tinge of gasoline from ski boats now docked. It's been a busy day on the water. Boats running at full speed down the length of the lake. Jet Skis rollicking in their wakes, their churning engines so tiresome when one isn't the rider. Laughter and shouts filling the air. Hollering and cheering. It's a joyful din, but by afternoon's end, I'm weary of it.

I sit, eating my dinner, watching the lake empty of its inhabitants as the sun falls in the sky to the west. One by one they leave, and I breathe a sigh of relief with each departure.

> *Take a deep breath in...and out, imagining yourself there, eating dinner, appreciating the peace of evening.*

Each morning I wake to the water cresting in foot-high whitecaps that crash on shore, as if intent on washing and washing and washing away the night. But I eat dinner each night beside water that stills to a near mirror perfection. On the other side of the lake, I see each branch of the bordering forest's trees reflected in the water's wavering glass.

It's that time of evening when the light is simply perfect. The fading sun shoots sheaves of harvest gold through the green pines, making them a heavenly color not seen in the brightness of noon. Down the lake, the Master paints the mountain peaks in a glorious purple and pink as if showing off for those aware.

When all the motorboats and Jet Skis are done for the day, their inhabitants trudging up to firepits and rustic kitchens for dinner, the lake is finally quiet. Finally, in a sense, mine again.

Consider the silence of the lake. The gentle murmur of your nearest neighbors in conversation, a sudden laugh carrying across the water. Imagine the smell. The scent of fuel, from a neighbor's boat prepared for the next day, washed away by the tiniest breeze through the trees of pine. The water—always the earthy, loamy, aqueous smell of the lake. These are smells you would know anywhere, helping you recognize the place you love.

Now there's no one on the lake save a man in the back of a canoe. He reverently, slowly strokes on one side, then the other, the lone worthy passenger for a time such as this. His tiny silhouette reflects in the water beside him, from hat to hand.

Take another moment to truly see yourself in this place, the sights and sounds and smells surrounding you. Deep breathe in...and out.

After watching the sun's skirt hem fade from hot amber hues to the pale lemon of twilight, the remains of my dinner drying on my plate, I enter the small cabin to don a sweater and long pants. My nearest neighbors are quiet. Perhaps they've abandoned the deck for the warmth and comfort of the cabin. But I will not. This night calls to me, begs me to return. Alone.

Across the lake I can see the flame of a flickering bonfire. I deem this a worthy goal, so I gather dried driftwood and pine cones and needles to start a fire in the center of large rocks that form a pit. Pulling matches from a waterproof box in the musty smelling boathouse, I strike one and watch its red-blue flame burst into brief fireworks before it dulls to a languid, rolling flicker. I crouch and set this flame among the needles. It smolders a bit, then catches, a crawling, waving movement as it eats away at the trees' fodder.

I blow quietly on the tiny fire, urging it onward, wary of putting it out. But the flame moves quickly through the brown needles parched by summer, moving on to the bigger prey of driftwood kindling. I gather other sticks on the beach, piling half-inch-thick wood in tepee fashion over the fire, then inch-thick branches. Soon I forage for wood of two to three inches diameter, then half-logs from a lodge pole pine with roots that yielded to winter's encroaching ice and had to be harvested with saw and axe.

With the fire roaring before me, happily sated for the moment, I sit in an old Adirondack chair, peeling of paint, splintering from too many winters. I stare and stare and stare at the wonder of fire.

> *See yourself there, watching the fire dance and flicker and pop as pitch meets heat. Let your inner eye rove from glowing ember to the pointy tips of the flames.*

It's getting colder as the twilight fades to the west, but my fire is warm. I edge the heavy chair forward a bit, risking the sparks, and rest my shoes on the firepit rocks. The rocks have been hewn by glaciers, warmed in the sun, split by ice. They absorb the heat of the fire.

Sitting alone, I consider the wonder of God's hand in the elements about me. Everywhere I look, it's as if for the first time.

I see His hand in the dark blue peaks in the distance, mighty and strong and thousands of years old.

In the beauty of the stilling lake, nature's mirror.

In the warmth and mystery of the forest surrounding me, meeting my hungry gaze across the water.

In His provision of heat to warm us and cook our food.

In His provision of clean water to slake our thirst.
In the wonder of His creation.

Imagine yourself in this place, fully comprehending
the magnitude of the Father's creation, everywhere you look.

I pour myself a cup of steaming decaf from the carafe beside me, sitting, I discover, at a precarious angle among the beach's rough rocks. I lean forward, welcoming the dry, hot sting of heat from the fire on my face, even as the back of my head chills. I cradle the warm cup between my cold fingers.

"Thank You, Father," I murmur. "Thank You for all You've given me. Thank You for the beauty of Your creation. For the sun and the earth and the water. For allowing me here."

My eyes move from the bright fire to the darkness of the lake, slowly adjusting. There's nobody about. The bonfire on the other side of the lake is low to the ground, its caretakers obviously more intent now on warm beds than continuing to feed the flames. My own fire has reached the tops of the logs, now eating as quickly downward as upward from the coals that are iron-bending hot.

As the drier bark and last rings of life are burned off, the flames dim and set to work on the marrow of the wood. This suits me, this almost complete union of fire and fuel.

I, too, am getting sleepy, my brain starting to think more of the warmth of down comforters in my bedroom than the warmth of this fire.

But the flickering glow transfixes me, the embers seemingly alive as they burst in a soundless hum of brightness, then dimming, then brightness again. From colors of white-red to brick, then white again.

I pull on a jacket against the night's stark chill. When I gaze across the lake again, there's no answering color of a shared fire, my neighbors electing to douse the embers and head to bed. It's late. Because there's no moon tonight, I can't determine the exact time, but I guess around eleven-thirty. The peekaboo cabin lights, emerging from between trees all along the lake, have been doused as well.

I imagine myself alone on this shore, seeing the lake as the native Indians once saw her. Pristine. Untouched. Exactly as God had shaped her. I long to travel back in time and see it as they saw it, but tonight, tonight it's close. I can see myself alone here.

The last two logs fall in on each other, their bridge now only so many fist-sized embers. The heat of the fire's foundation will make short work of them, but still I stare, finding it as hard to leave its edge as it is to shut off an engrossing movie on a seldom-watched channel.

I understand that what keeps me here is mostly this feeling of solidarity with the Creator, of acknowledging His hand in all things about me, in the silence of the lake I so often must share.

He is here. He is here. He is here.

With me. Hovering above me and sitting in the other aged, peeling, splintering Adirondack beside me—and out on the dock—and inside me. Me, of all people.

> *Take a moment to consider the moment when you first understood*
> *that the Creator of all is with you too. The Creator—who can*
> *shove mountains from their earthly lair, who can fill valleys with*
> *glaciers and melt them, who can surround us with seas and pristine*
> *white beaches and miles of fertile prairie lands—is with you.*
> *As interested in you as He is in the formation of the planet.*
> *Consider the magnitude of this thought. Talk to Him about it.*

I watch and watch my bonfire burning away, the chill staved off a bit as I think of my Father's robe about me. I think of forgiveness, wholeness, how He knit me together in my mother's womb, and how He brought me here to this place. And the wonder that He considers me special enough to walk beside me.

The fire's nearly out. I rise and grab an old pail. I crouch at the water's edge and dip, filling the metal bucket. I douse and drown the embers, watching white steam rise, the blackness of night suddenly that much closer. But this time isn't over for me.

As my eyes adjust to the night, the fire gone for the day,

I notice for the first time the wonder of the sky. From the fire's edge, while watching sparks embark on a final, frantic flight, I'd seen the myriad stars covering the night above me. But now, with no competing light, I see for the first time the wonder of God's canvas. The millions of stars and planets and supernovas, the broad sweeping path of the Milky Way.

I drop my pail and walk out onto the dock, the chill of the water making me pull my jacket closer. I grab a towel from my boat, then continue out to the very end of the dock. Lying down, placing the towel under my head as a pillow, I hear the gentle wash of the water. My eyes hungrily search the sky.

There are satellites tracking in steady, quick paths around the circumference of Earth. Spy satellites and television satellites and cell phone satellites. The creations of humankind are in themselves, amazing. But the wonder of Cassiopeia and Andromeda and the Big Dipper, the red twinkling light of Jupiter, the cool blue light of Venus, the millions upon millions of stars that make up the ivory ribbon of the Milky Way—now this, this is truly amazing.

I stare upward until I spot a shooting star and then another. I grin and whisper a prayer of thanks, as if God had sent them down just for me, like a father for a child on the Fourth of July.

"Thank You for this night, this peace, this wonder," I whisper upward.

*Silently thank your Father now for the wonder
of His creation, wherever you are.*

A chill rolls down my neck and I widen my eyes. I feel warmed from the inside out. God is nearing me again, allowing me to sense His presence. Or maybe I'm simply in the right place, allowing myself to know what I have always known. He is near.

"Father?" I whisper.

Another star shoots across the sky, this time close enough that I sit up in wonder and alarm, wondering if it's coming down to Earth. But its brilliance is short-lived, and it quickly burns out and fades, like the fastest bonfire ever.

I cradle my knees to my chest and feel the breeze picking up on the lake, the nightly wash beginning to build. In the slight wind, I feel the Maker's movement. In the stars and the beauty of this place, I see His creation. For a brief moment, I can see beyond my own life—beyond my brief life span, beyond my normal self-absorbed world—to Him.

He is full of splendor.

Silently repeat this phrase and those to come.
"You are full of splendor, Lord."

He comes in awesome majesty.

"You are majestic, Lord."

He is at once beyond my reach and *right here*.

"You are more than I can imagine, Father."

He is exalted, holy.

"You are Most High, the God of the earth and all the heavens.

"Thank You, Lord, for this place, for my life,
for Your presence in both. Thank You for making me aware.
I bow at Your feet. I'm humbled that You would draw near me.
Help me to always be in awe of Your majesty, Father. Amen."

I smile and pull my jacket closer again, willing my body to stay warm enough to remain here, with my Lord, as long as I can. But the cold is too much for my weak flesh, and at last I rise and pad down the dock, dropping my towel into the boat. I pass the waterlogged firepit and then climb the stairs to the cabin.

As I nestle into my bed, covered by a down comforter, I stare out the window at the lake, her waves rising in the growing wind. I understand and remember that God is always with me, that He's at work within me, still creating and shaping my heart. If I let Him.

I think again of the wonder of the night sky, and I pray. "Father in heaven, help me let You mold me as You wish.

Make me as wondrous as the stars in the sky by making me more and more Your servant. Let me reflect Your light…"

Continue on with this prayer as you feel led.

I nestle deeper under the covers and allow myself the heavy, slow breathing of oncoming slumber. "Amen," I whisper. "So be it. Amen and amen and amen." ⚔

Dear Reader,

You get the idea now, this God-encounter thing. I have a God encounter every night when I pray. Usually, it's not an amazing, faith-exploding event, but more comfortable, easy. A handful of times it's been truly phenomenal.

I invite Jesus to come closer, right there into my bedroom, to sit beside me, to talk with me. I usually see him taking my hand, and I begin with a confession. Something on the order of, "Lord, I'm such a fool. Can you forgive an idiot like me?" And He pats my hand and shoots me a tender smile, then nods, laughter and delight in his eyes: total forgiveness. "Yes, Lisa. Yes, I can," I hear Him say. Then I go on to chat about my day, my life, my heart, and I sense Him listening, understanding, directing. Showing me more and more of His heart so I can better serve Him.

Unlike certain television programs, I encourage you to do this at home. Clear your mind of the menial things that crowd it. Draw away to a quiet place. Focus on your Lord, your God. Invite Him to draw near, to let you feel His presence. If it helps, see yourself someplace peaceful and inviting, like many of the places described in this book. Ask Him to bar the Evil One from your door, your mind, your heart. You want to feel only His presence—ask for His protection. Imagine Him coming closer, maybe a speck in the distance, walking toward you, ever toward you, and as He nears, you realize His eyes are only on you. Confess your sins; ask Him what you've longed to ask. Listen for His voice, that nudging in your heart, your gut, or the distinct words from His lips. See Him look at you, loving you, longing to make you His companion, servant, friend, and disciple in every way.

Fully encounter the living God.

Thoughts of all of you, out there, doing this, makes me smile. Knowing God better, perhaps, because of this book. Because of an idea God laid in my heart, spilled out of my mind and soul and fingers. Proof in itself that God can use any of us. He can use you, too: for great things, amazing things.

Go with God, my friends. No, I mean it. Actually *go* with Him. Feel Him take your hand, pull you along, push you into areas heretofore unknown. And look upon the face of Jesus. Trust Him. Learn more about Him. Turn to Scripture for a better grasp on who He was once, who He still is today. It only gets better from here.

In Him,

Lisa Tawn Bergren

www.GodEncounter.com